Maths Out Loud
Year 2

by
Sara Fielder

Acknowledgements

Jane Prothero and Woodlands Primary School, Leeds

Karen Holman and Paddox Primary School, Rugby

Heather Nixon and Gayhurst Primary School, Buckinghamshire

John Ellard and Kingsley Primary School, Northampton

Jackie Smith, Catherine Torr and Roberttown CE J & I School, Kirklees

Wendy Price and St Martin's CE Primary School, Wolverhampton

Helen Elis Jones, University of Wales, Bangor

Ruth Trundley, Devon Curriculum Services, Exeter

Trudy Lines and Bibury CE Primary School, Gloucestershire

Elaine Folen and St Paul's Infant School, Surrey

Jane Airey and Frith Manor Primary School, Barnet

Beverley Godfrey, South Wales Home Educators' Network

Kay Brunsdon and Gwyrosydd Infant School, Swansea

Keith Cadman, Wolverhampton Advisory Services

Helen Andrews and Blue Coat School, Birmingham

Oakridge Parochial School, Gloucestershire

The Islington BEAM Development Group

Published by BEAM Education

Maze Workshops

72a Southgate Road

London N1 3JT

Telephone 020 7684 3323

Fax 020 7684 3334

Email info@beam.co.uk

www.beam.co.uk

© Beam Education 2006

All rights reserved. None of the material in this
book may be reproduced in any form without prior
permission of the publisher

ISBN 1 903142 84 9

British Library Cataloguing-in-Publication Data

Data available

Edited by Marion Dill

Designed by Malena Wilson-Max

Photographs by Len Cross

Thanks to Rotherfield Primary School

Printed in England by Cromwell Press Ltd

Contents

Introduction

Language plays an important part in the learning of mathematics – especially oral language. Children's relationship to the subject, their grasp of it and sense of ownership all depend on discussion and interaction – as do the social relationships that provide the context for learning. A classroom where children talk about mathematics is one that will help build their confidence and transform their whole attitude to learning.

Why is speaking and listening important in maths?

- Talking is creative. In expressing thoughts and discussing ideas, children actually shape these ideas, make connections and hone their definitions of what words mean.
- You cannot teach what a word means – you can only introduce it, explain it, then let children try it out, misuse it, see when it works and how it fits with what they already know and, eventually, make it their own.
- Speaking and listening to other children involves and motivates children – they are more likely to learn and remember than when engaging silently with a textbook or worksheet.
- As you listen to children, you identify children's misconceptions and realise which connections (between bits of maths) they have not yet made.

How does this book help me include 'speaking and listening' in maths?

- The lessons are structured to use and develop oral language skills in mathematics. Each lesson uses one or more classroom techniques that foster the use of spoken language and listening skills.
- The grid on p17 shows those speaking and listening objectives that are suitable for developing through the medium of mathematics. Each lesson addresses one of these objectives.
- The lessons draw on a bank of classroom techniques which are described on p8. These techniques are designed to promote children's use of speaking and listening in a variety of ways.

How does 'using and applying mathematics' fit in with these lessons?

- Many of the mathematical activities in this book involve problem solving, communication and reasoning, all key areas of 'using and applying mathematics' (U&A). Where this aspect of a lesson is particularly significant, this is acknowledged and expanded on in one of the 'asides' to the main lesson.

What about children with particular needs?

- For children who have impaired hearing, communication is particularly important, as it is all too easy for them to become isolated from their peers. Speaking and listening activities, even if adapted, simplified or supported by an assistant, help such children be a part of their learning community and to participate in the curriculum on offer.

- Children who speak English as an additional language benefit from speaking and listening activities, especially where these are accompanied by diagrams, drawings or the manipulation of numbers or shapes, which help give meaning to the language. Check that they understand the key words needed for the topic being discussed and, where possible, model the activity, paying particular attention to the use of these key words. Remember to build in time for thinking and reflecting on oral work.

- Differences in children's backgrounds affect the way they speak to their peers and adults. The lessons in this book can help children acquire a rich repertoire of ways to interact and work with others. Children who are less confident with written forms can develop confidence through speaking and listening.

- Gender can be an issue in acquiring and using speaking and listening skills. Girls may be collaborative and tentative, while boys sometimes can be more assertive about expressing their ideas. Address such differences by planning different groups, partners, classroom seating and activities. These lessons build on children's strengths and challenge them in areas where they are less strong.

What are the 'personal skills' learning objectives?

- There is a range of personal and social skills that children need to develop across the curriculum and throughout their school career. These include enquiry skills, creative thinking skills and ways of working with others. Some are particularly relevant to the maths classroom, and these are listed on the grid on p18.

What about assessment?

- Each lesson concludes with a section called 'Assessment for learning', which offers suggestions for what to look out for during the lesson and questions to ask in order to assess children's learning of all three learning objectives. There is also help on what may lie behind children's failure to meet these objectives and suggestions for teaching that might rectify the situation.

- Each section of four lessons includes a sheet of self-assessment statements to be printed from the accompanying CD-ROM and to be filled in at the end of each lesson or when all four are completed. Display the sheet and also give children their own copies. Then go through the statements, discussing and interpreting them as necessary. Ask children to complete their self-assessments with a partner they frequently work with. They should each fill in their own sheet, then look at it with their partner who adds their own viewpoint.

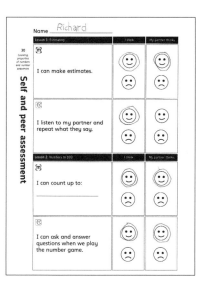

How can I make the best use of these lessons?

- Aim to develop a supportive classroom climate, where all ideas are accepted and considered, even if they may seem strange or incorrect. You will need to model this yourself in order for children to see what acceptance and open-mindedness look like.
- Create an ethos of challenge, where children are required to think about puzzles and questions.
- Slow down. Don't expect answers straight away when you ask questions. Build in thinking time where you do not communicate with the children, so that they have to reflect on their answers before making them. Expect quality rather than quantity.
- Model the language of discussion. Children who may be used to maths being either 'correct' or 'incorrect' need to learn by example what debate means. Choose a debating partner from the class, or work with another adult, and demonstrate uncertainty, challenge, exploration, questioning ...
- Tell children what they will be learning in the lesson. Each lesson concludes with an 'Assessment for learning' section offering suggestions for what to look out for to assess children's learning of all three learning objectives. Share these with the children at the start of the lesson to involve them in their own learning process.

How should I get the best out of different groupings?

- Get children used to working in a range of different groupings: pairs, threes or fours or as a whole class.
- Organise pairs in different ways on different occasions: familiar maths partners (who can communicate well); pairs of friends (who enjoy working together); children of differing abilities (who can learn something from each other); someone they don't know (to get them used to talking and listening respectfully to any other person).
- Give children working in pairs and groups some time for independent thought and work.
- Support pairs when they prepare to report back to the class. Go over with them what they have done or discovered and what they might say about this. Help them make brief notes – just single words or phrases – to remind them what they are going to say. If you are busy, ask an assistant or another child to take over your role. Then, when it comes to feedback time, support them by gentle probes or questions: "What did you do next?" or "What do your notes say?"

Classroom techniques used in this book

Ways of working

Peer tutoring
pairs of children

good for

This technique can benefit both the child who is being 'taught' and also the 'tutor' who develops a clearer understanding of what they themselves have learned and, in explaining it, can make new connections and solidify old ones. Children often make the best teachers, because they are close to the state of not knowing and can remember what helped them bridge the gap towards understanding.

how to organise it

'Peer tutoring' can work informally – children work in mixed ability pairs, and if one child understands an aspect of the work that the other doesn't, they work together in a tutor/pupil relationship to make sure the understanding is shared by both. Alternatively, you can structure it more formally. Observe children at work and identify those who are confident and accurate with the current piece of mathematics. Give them the title of 'Expert' and ask them to work with individuals needing support. Don't overuse this: the tutor has a right to work and learn at their own level, and tutoring others should only play a small part in their school lives.

Talking partners
pairs of children

good for

This technique helps children develop and practise the skills of collaboration in an unstructured way. Children can articulate their thinking, listen to one another and support each other's learning in a 'safe' situation.

how to organise it

Pairs who have previously worked together (for example, 'One between two', below) work together informally. The children in these pairs have had time to build up trust between them, and should have the confidence to tackle a new, less structured task. If you regularly use 'Talking partners', pairs of children will get used to working together. This helps them develop confidence, but runs the risk that children mutually reinforce their misunderstandings. In this case, changing partners occasionally can bring fresh life to the class by creating new meetings of minds.

One between two
pairs of children

good for

This technique helps children develop their skills of explaining, questioning and listening – behaviours that are linked to positive learning outcomes. Use it when the children have two or more problems or calculations to solve.

how to organise it

Pairs share a pencil (or calculator or other tool), and each assumes one of two roles: 'Solver' or 'Recorder'. (Supplying just one pencil encourages children to stay in role by preventing the Solver from making their own notes.)

The Solver has a problem and works through it out loud. The Recorder keeps a written record of what the Solver is doing. If the Solver needs something written down or a calculation done on the calculator, they must ask the Recorder to do this for them. If the Recorder is not sure of what the Solver is doing, they ask for further explanations, but do not engage in actually solving the problem. After each problem, children swap roles.

Introduce this way of working by modelling it yourself with a confident child partner: you talk through your own method of solving a problem, and the child records this thought process on the board.

Barrier games

pairs of children

good for

These techniques help children focus on spoken language rather than gesture or facial expression. The children must listen carefully to what is said, because they cannot see the person speaking.

how to organise it

Barrier games focus on giving and receiving instructions. Pairs of children work with a book or screen between them, so that they cannot see each other's work. The speaker gives information or instructions to the listener. The listener, in turn, asks questions to clarify understanding and gain information.

Eyes closed, eyes open

any number of children

good for

Depending on how this technique is used, it can either encourage children to listen carefully, because they cannot rely on visual checks, or to look carefully, because something was changed while they were not looking and they now need to identify this change.

how to organise it

Do this with the class: ask them to close their eyes while you count (slipping in a deliberate error) or drop coins into a tin. They must listen carefully to identify what you have done. Children then can do a similar activity in pairs.

Or tell children to close their eyes while you make one change in a sequence of numbers, pattern of shapes or some other structured set. When children open their eyes, they must spot what you have done and describe it or instruct you how to undo the change. Again, pairs can then carry on doing this independently.

Rotating roles
groups of various sizes

good for

Working in a small group to solve a problem encourages children to articulate their thinking and support each other's learning.

how to organise it

Careful structuring discourages individuals from taking the lead too often. Assign different roles to the children in the group: Chairperson, Reader, Recorder, Questioner, and so on. Over time, everyone has a turn at each role. You may wish to give children 'role labels' to remind them of their current role.

When you introduce this technique, model the role of chairperson in a group, with the rest of the class watching. Show how to include everyone and then discuss with the children what you have done, so as to make explicit techniques that they can use.

Discussion

Think, pair, share
groups of four

good for

Putting pairs together to work as a group of four helps avoid the situation where children in pairs mutually reinforce their common misunderstandings. It gives children time to think on their own, rehearse their thoughts with a partner and then discuss in a larger group. This encourages everyone to join in and discourages the 'quick thinkers' from dominating a discussion.

how to organise it

The technique is a development of 'Tell your partner' and involves the following:
- One or two minutes for individuals to think about a problem or statement and, possibly, to jot down their initial thoughts
- Two or three minutes where individuals work in pairs to share their thoughts
- Four or five minutes for two pairs to join together and discuss
- If you wish, you can also allow ten minutes for reporting back from some or all groups and whole-class discussion.

You can vary this pattern and the timings, but always aim to give children some 'private' thinking time.

Talking stick
any number of children

good for

Giving all children a turn at speaking and being listened to.

how to organise it

Provide the class with decorated sticks, which confer status on whoever holds them. Then, in a small or large group (or even the whole class), make it the rule that only the person holding the stick may speak, while the other children listen. You can use the stick in various ways: pass it around the circle; tell the child with the stick to pass it to whoever they want to speak next; have a chairperson who decides who will hold the stick next; ask the person with the stick to repeat what the previous person said before adding their own comments or ideas.

Tell your partner

pairs

good for

Whole-class question-and-answer sessions favour the quick and the confident and do not provide time and space for slower thinkers. This technique involves all children in answering questions and in discussion.

how to organise it

Do this in one of two ways:
- When you have just asked a question or presented an idea to think about, ask each child to turn to their neighbour or partner and tell them the answer. They then take turns to speak and to listen.
- Work less formally, simply asking children to talk over their ideas with a partner. Children may find this sharing difficult at first. They may not value talking to another child, preferring to talk to the teacher or not expressing their ideas at all. In this case, do some work on listening skills such as timing 'a minute each way' or repeating back to their partner what they have just said.

Devil's advocate

any number of children

good for

Statements – false or ambiguous as well as true – are often better than questions at provoking discussion.

how to organise it

In discussion with children, take the role of 'Devil's advocate', in which you make statements for them to agree or disagree with and to argue about.
To avoid confusing children by making false statements yourself, mention 'a friend' or 'someone you know' who makes these statements (a version of the 'silly teddy' who, in Nursery and Reception, makes mistakes for the children to correct). Alternatively, explain that when you make statements with your hands behind your back, your fingers may be crossed and you may be saying things that are not true.

Reporting back

Ticket to explain

individuals

good for

This is a way of structuring feedback which helps children get the maximum out of offering explanations to the class. Everyone hears a method explained twice, and children have to listen carefully to their peers, rather than simply think about their own method.

how to organise it

When individuals want to explain their method of working to the class, their 'ticket' to be able to do this is to re-explain the method demonstrated by the child immediately before them. Or children work with a partner and explain their ideas to each other. When called on to speak, they explain their partner's idea and then their own.

1, 2, 3, 4

groups of four

good for

This technique offers the same benefits as 'Heads or tails', but is used for groups of four children rather than pairs.

how to organise it

This is a technique identical to 'Heads or tails', but with groups of four. Instead of tossing a coin, children are numbered 1 to 4, and the speaker is chosen by the roll of a dice (if 5 or 6 come up, simply roll again).

Tell the class

individuals

good for

Encouraging children who lack skills or confidence to speak in front of the class.

how to organise it

In a plenary (or mini-plenary held during the course of a lesson), invite children to the front and support them in talking to the class by asking questions for them to answer. Gradually, experiences such as this can give children confidence to make their own statements.

Heads or tails

pairs of children

good for

When pairs of children work together, one child may rely heavily on the other to make decisions and to communicate or one child may take over, despite the efforts of the other child to have a say. This technique encourages pairs to work together to understand something and helps prevent an uneven workload.

how to organise it

Invite pairs to the front of the class to explain their ideas or solutions. When they get to the front, ask them to nominate who is heads and who is tails, then toss a coin to decide which of them does the talking. They have one opportunity to 'ask a friend' (probably their partner). As all children in the class know that they may be chosen to speak in this way, because the toss of the coin could make either of them into the 'explainer', they are motivated to work with their partner to reach a common understanding. Assigning the choice of explainer to the toss of a coin stops children feeling that anyone is picking on them personally (do warn them in advance, though!). Variation: If a pair of children has different ideas on a topic, ask both to offer explanations of each other's ideas.

Additional techniques

Below are some further classroom techniques that are referred to in the lessons in this book.

Ideas map

whole class

good for

This technique enables children to identify what they know and what they don't know and so equips them to monitor their own learning.

Drawing up an ideas map at the start of teaching a topic can produce valuable material on which to base initial assessments of the children's understanding. It also serves to steer the children towards what they will be learning. Return to the map and even revise and adapt it after a period of teaching in order to consolidate children's learning.

how to organise it

Develop your first ideas maps as a whole class. Hold a creative brainstorm with the children to conjure up as many terms connected to a topic as they can think of, with you adding more terms as appropriate – scribe the contributions and, as you do so, prompt the children to help you establish connections between them.

Once children are used to the idea, they can work in groups or as individuals to draw up ideas maps of their own. They can either work from scratch or you can start them off with a whole-class creative brainstorm, where you collect terms but don't make any connections. Children then devise their own ideas map, using some or all of these terms.

When they construct the map, children aim to link terms together and write on the links something to describe the nature of the connection. Some teachers ask children to write individual words or phrases on sticky notes, so that they can move them around and explore different links before settling on the ones they want to describe.

Chewing the fat

any number of children

good for

Leaving ideas or questions unresolved provides thoughtful children with the opportunity to extend their thinking and can help develop good habits. Many real mathematicians like to have problems to think about in odd moments, just as some people like crossword clues or chess moves to occupy their mind.

how to organise it

Sometimes end a lesson with ideas, problems or challenges for children to ponder in their own time as you may have run out of time or one of the children has come up with a question or an idea which can only be discussed the next day.

Reframing

any number of children

good for

'Reframing' alters the meaning of something by altering its context or description. It helps children find their way into a difficult or new idea by hearing it rephrased and enlarged.

how to organise it

Rephrase children's words using a variety of language: "You read that out as 'twenty-five multiplied by seven'. That means seven lots of 25." After a few seconds, say: "Imagine a pile of 25 beans, and you've got seven piles like that."

Charts

Classroom techniques

This chart shows which of the classroom techniques previously described are used in which lessons.

	COUNTING, PROPERTIES OF NUMBERS AND NUMBER SEQUENCES	PLACE VALUE AND ORDERING	CALCULATIONS	HANDLING DATA	MEASURES	SHAPE AND SPACE
	Lesson	Lesson	Lesson	Lesson	Lesson	Lesson
One between two		8				
Talking partners	4		10, 12	16	18	22
Rotating roles						23
Peer tutoring		6, 7			17	
Eyes closed, eyes open	1			14		
Barrier games						21
Talking stick	2	5			19	
Tell your partner				13		24
Devil's advocate				15		
Think, pair, share					20	
Heads or tails / 1, 2, 3, 4	3		11			
Tell the class			9			

Speaking and listening skills

This chart shows which speaking and listening skills are practised in which lessons.

	COUNTING, PROPERTIES OF NUMBERS AND NUMBER SEQUENCES	PLACE VALUE AND ORDERING	CALCULATIONS	HANDLING DATA	MEASURES	SHAPE AND SPACE
	Lesson	Lesson	Lesson	Lesson	Lesson	Lesson
Talk about shared work with a partner	4		10	14	18	24
Reach a common understanding with a partner		7	11	16		22
Speak confidently in front of the class			9		19	
Give accurate instructions					17	21
Explain and justify thinking				13		
Contribute to small-group and whole-class discussion	3		12	15	20	23
Listen and follow instructions accurately		5				
Listen to others and ask relevant questions	1, 2	8				
Listen with sustained concentration		6				

Personal skills

This chart shows which personal skills are practised in which lessons.

	COUNTING, PROPERTIES OF NUMBERS AND NUMBER SEQUENCES	PLACE VALUE AND ORDERING	CALCULATIONS	HANDLING DATA	MEASURES	SHAPE AND SPACE
	Lesson	Lesson	Lesson	Lesson	Lesson	Lesson
Organise work						
Identify stages in the process of fulfilling a task					18	
Check work	4	8	9	14		
Organise findings	3		10	15		
Work with others						
Work cooperatively with others	2	5				22, 23
Overcome difficulties and recover from mistakes		6				24
Show awareness and understanding of others' needs					17	
Improve learning and performance						
Reflect on learning		7	11, 12			
Critically evaluate own work						21
Take pride in work				13	19	
Develop confidence in own judgements	1			16	20	

Lessons

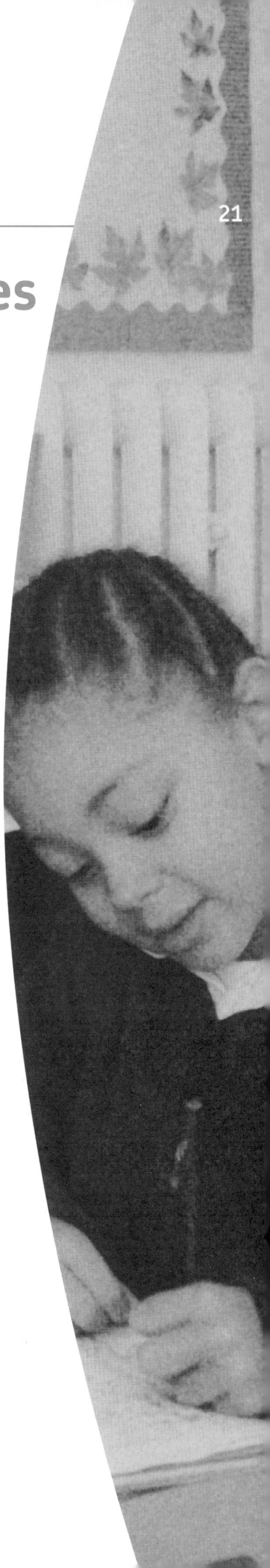

Counting, properties of numbers and number sequences

Learning objectives

	Lessons			
	1	2	3	4
ⓜ Maths objectives				
use and begin to read the vocabulary of estimation and approximation	●			
count forwards to 100 and back again		●		
recognise odd and even numbers to 30			●	
count reliably up to 100 objects by grouping them in tens, fives and twos				●
Ⓢ Speaking and listening skills				
listen to others and ask relevant questions	●	●		
contribute to small-group discussion			●	
talk about shared work with a partner				●
Ⓟ Personal skills				
improve learning and performance: develop confidence in own judgements	●			
work with others: work cooperatively with others		●		
organise work: organise findings			●	
organise work: check work				●

About these lessons

Lesson 1: Estimating

 Use and begin to read the vocabulary of estimation and approximation

There is a huge conceptual difference between counting in order to get an accurate answer and estimating an amount. Children need experience of both. In this lesson, they estimate a number of shapes, using visual clues, and talk about how they made the estimate.

 Listen to others and ask relevant questions

Classroom technique: Eyes closed, eyes open

Children close their eyes while you alter the number of objects on view, then open them to estimate the new number. The new number of objects is displayed only briefly, so children must develop strategies for estimating the number.

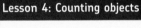 **Improve learning and performance: develop confidence in own judgements**

Once children understand that exact answers are not required, they can begin to make 'informed guesses' about the number of objects. As they gain experience and make more realistic estimates, children develop confidence in their abilities in this area.

Lesson 2: Numbers to 100

 Count forwards to 100 and back again

This lesson makes links between mathematics and PE. Children move around a large space, asking and answering mathematical questions to work out the number on their forehead. Children then work out the sequence of numbers represented by the class and put themselves in order accordingly.

Listen to others and ask relevant questions

Classroom technique: Talking stick

The child with the 'talking stick' has a special status as they may give instructions to the whole class. To understand and follow these instructions, the other children must listen carefully.

Work with others: work cooperatively with others

The whole class share a task and must cooperate to fulfil it. The task is a playful one, which gives children a further incentive to work together well.

Lesson 3: Odd and even numbers

Recognise odd and even numbers to 30

Children sort numbers into odd and even and make a general statement about how they can tell whether a number is odd or even.

 Contribute to small-group discussion

Classroom technique: 1, 2, 3, 4

When the class prepare for the plenary, children are told that any one of them could be chosen to make the presentation. This ensures that all children discuss the presentation and avoids the group relying on one child to make the decisions and other members taking a back seat.

 Organise work: organise findings

Part of the group's task is to organise and record their work before showing it to the class in the plenary. Children can be quite creative about this – for example, cutting out numbers to stick in boxes drawn on paper or writing out numbers with different-coloured pens.

Lesson 4: Counting objects

Count reliably up to 100 objects by grouping them in tens, fives and twos

Counting a collection in ones can take a long time and result in errors. This lesson looks at developing quicker and more efficient strategies for counting numbers of coins.

 Talk about shared work with a partner

Classroom technique: Talking partners

Children work together informally, agreeing estimates, discussing which strategies to use for counting and carrying out the counting.

 Organise work: check work

Children are encouraged to check that they counted accurately, as another pair will also be counting the same set of objects and expect to reach the same conclusion.

Estimating
Classroom technique: Eyes closed, eyes open

24

Learning objectives

(m) Maths
Use and begin to read the vocabulary of estimation and approximation

Speaking and listening
'Listen to others and ask them questions'
Listen to others and ask relevant questions

Personal skills
'Develop confidence about what you think and decide'
Improve learning and performance: develop confidence in own judgements

(w) Words and phrases
guess, how many, estimate, roughly, close to, exact, about the same as, answer, explain

(r) Resources
large dice
display copy of RS1

Introduction

Show children a dice face for a few seconds. Children look at the spots, then turn to their neighbour and explain the number of spots they saw and the arrangement – for example, "I saw two groups of two and one in the middle"; "I saw four and one in the middle." Repeat with another dice face.

(m) *What do you think you saw?*

Was your partner's explanation clear? Do you need to ask them to explain it again?

Pairs/Whole class

Display RS1. Reveal the shapes briefly. Working in pairs, children estimate how many shapes they saw in total. Pairs discuss their estimates and their methods for doing this.

A few children report back their partner's estimate and strategy. Accept all answers and record all estimates on the board, in order.

13	20	40	72

As a class, count the shapes (there are 22). Help the class calculate the difference between the closest estimate and the exact amount.

> There were 22 shapes.
> Estimate 20.
> 20   21   22
> The difference was 2.

Children close their eyes while you cover some of the shapes or add some more, then open them and view RS1 briefly. They discuss with their partner whether the number of objects is more or less than before and approximately how many there were.

Show the adapted sheet again, discuss the estimates made as a class and, again, calculate the difference between the closest estimate and the exact amount.

Repeat the activity, changing or adding shapes.

Listen to others and ask relevant questions
Encourage children to question their partners further if explanations are not clear.

Develop confidence
Making an estimate can feel risky for children who are more used to trying for accurate answers. Accepting all estimates and emphasising that there is no correct answer can help children develop the confidence to 'have a go'.

Difference
Encourage children to work out the difference between their own estimate and the actual number, but don't insist on this if you think it might sap their confidence.

Did you explain to your partner how you made your estimate?

Are you getting better at making estimates? How do you know?

Support: Ask children leading questions such as "Do you think there were more than 10 shapes? More than 100?" and provide a number line so children have a visual image of numbers in order.

Extend: Children continue doing similar activities in pairs: one child shows a handful of objects for the count of 5 while their partner estimates. They then count the objects together.

Plenary

Playfulness
Activities such as this can help develop the idea that maths is not just about correct answers and that, sometimes, exact answers are not even possible – how could you possibly count the birds in the sky?

Take the class outside or look out of the classroom window. Pairs discuss and provide an estimate for one or more of the following:

> the number of trees along the street/in the school field
>
> the number of birds flying overhead
>
> the number of cars travelling along the road (this would present a greater challenge if the cars cannot be seen and children have to rely on aural clues only)
>
> the length of the playground in metres or strides

Approximately how many trees are there on this side of the field? And on that side?

Tell your partner why you think the playground is more than 100 metres long.

Assessment for learning

Can the children

Make a reasonable estimate of up to 30 objects?

Listen to their partner and repeat back what they said in front of the class?

Speak confidently when offering an estimate?

If not

Do more work on counting sets of objects to develop a feel for what various quantities look like.

Encourage careful listening by playing games such as 'Simon says', where the leader says something and the children repeat it only if the phrase was preceded by the words 'Simon says'.

Confirm children's judgements, emphasising the approximate nature of estimates: "There are a lot more shapes this time, so 30 is a sensible estimate. Well done!"

Numbers to 100
Classroom technique: Talking stick

Learning objectives

Maths
Count forwards to 100 and back again

Speaking and listening
'Listen to others and ask them questions'
Listen to others and ask relevant questions

Personal skills
'Work well with others'
Work with others: work cooperatively with others

Words and phrases
forwards, backwards, up, down, before, after, count, sequence, check, correct, question

Resources
'talking stick'
sticky notes with numbers written on
100-grid or number line

Kinaesthetic counting
Counting movements stimulates the brain because it requires multitasking – verbalising number sequences while moving to the count.

Playing the game
Be strict about the rules: explain that the game only works if you do not look at your own number. Support children by suggesting questions: "Does my number have two digits?"; "Is my number over 50?"

U&A Use reasoning and logic
Children must draw inferences from negative as well as positive answers. If the answer to "Is my number over 50?" is "No", they need to work out which numbers to eliminate. Show how to use a 100-grid or a number line to record the information gleaned.

Introduction

This lesson is most effective in a large space such as the hall or playground.

The class start counting to 100, slowly and in unison. At a given number, call 'stop'. Children continue counting, but, for each number, do a movement (star jump, clap hands, arms wide, nod the head).

Give one child the 'talking stick'. They call 'stop' and request a different movement to accompany the counting. The child then passes the stick on and joins in the counting.

Repeat the process until the class reach 100, then do the same as children count backwards to zero.

 We counted to 36. What comes next?

Can you think of a movement that everybody can manage?

Whole class

Children close their eyes. Place a sticky note with a number written on on every child's forehead, making sure that children don't see their own number. Use numbers 0 to 30, or 10 to 45, or 50 to 80.

Children start to move around the class. When you call 'stop', they turn to the child next to them and ask one question about the number on their head. The other child must not tell them the number, but answers the question.

When a child guesses their number correctly, they come to the front to watch the others. Give one of these children the 'talking stick' to choose when to stop the game for the next question and answer.

Continue until most children know their number.

Give the 'talking stick' to three children. They have three minutes to instruct the class to position themselves so that all their numbers are in order. If they are successful, the class count up and back in the correct order. If unsuccessful, the 'talking stick' passes to another three children.

Finally, recite the sequence, one child at a time saying their number.

(m) *What do you notice about the numbers on children's foreheads? Which is the lowest number?*

(face) *What have you learned about your number so far?*

(face) *Why would it spoil things if we told people what their numbers are?*

Support: Give children a low number. Children may ask two questions at each 'stop'.

Extend: Mingle with the children yourself and provide additional, challenging clues – for example, "Your number is in the 4 times table." Work with just odd or just even numbers.

Plenary

Children find the person with the number that is two more than theirs, which will result in separate chains of children with odd and even numbers to form.

Each chain recites the sequence, one child at a time saying their number.

Finish off the lesson by counting to 100 and back.

(face) *How will you know when to say your number? What number are you listening out for?*

(face) *How can you help your group?*

Assessment for learning

Can the children	If not
(m) Count to 100 forwards and then back?	(m) Support children's counting by pointing to each number on a 100-grid. Practise this often so it becomes habitual to children.
(face) Ask questions to guess their own number?	(face) Stop the activity and briefly brainstorm a list of helpful questions for children to ask.
(face) Take turns when asking and answering questions?	(face) Play 'loop' games with the whole class to develop skills in listening and giving space for other people to speak.

Odd and even numbers

Classroom technique: 1, 2, 3, 4

Even
Reinforce the idea that all even numbers are multiples of 2.

Tell your partner
Children take turns with a partner to say an even number (that will be red) and an odd number (that won't be red).

Odd and even
Look for different explanations: "All the numbers in the 2 column are even"; "If numbers end in 4, they are even"; "Odd numbers are the ones that don't end in an even number."

Equal participation
If necessary, discuss with the group how to ensure each child is involved – for example, taking turns to choose a number to sort.

Organising the task
Encourage children to be creative. They may want to cut out the numbers and stick them in boxes drawn on paper or write out the numbers with different-coloured pens. Provide materials to facilitate these or other options.

Introduction

Explain that the class will be looking at numbers which are multiples of 2 and numbers which aren't. Revisit the definition of multiple: the 'family' of numbers you say when counting in twos, fives or tens from zero.

Display a 100-grid. The class count in unison from 0 in multiples of 2, stopping at 30, and count back. Colour the counted numbers in red on the grid.

Repeat, this time starting at an even number such as 24 or 64. As children count on, highlight the even numbers in red.

Return to an uncoloured 100-grid and ask children which squares will be red, and which won't, if you do the same with this grid.

As a class, discuss how you can tell which numbers are even and which are odd.

(m) *10, 20, 50 and 100 are multiples of 10. What other multiples of 10 do you know?*

(m) *Is 12 odd or even? How do you know?*

(s) *If a number isn't even, it is odd. Why is that?*

(s) *What can you say to your partner about the pattern? Which number would come next?*

Groups of three

Children work in groups of three, sharing a copy of RS2. They discuss how to sort the numbers into odd or even and then do so. Explain that part of the task is to work together to organise and record their work, as they will be showing it to the class in the plenary.

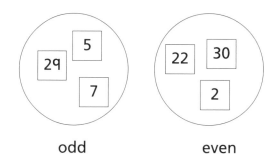

odd   even

Groups must also be prepared to present an explanation of how they can tell whether a number is odd or even in the plenary.

Preparing for the plenary
Tell the entire group to be prepared to report back, as any one of them could be chosen.

(m) *Which bit of the number do you need to look at to help you decide whether it is even?*

Tell Henry why you think that number belongs in the other set.

Will the rest of the class understand your explanation?

Support: Provide cards which can be manipulated. Help children check each number against the coloured 100-grid.

Extend: Children add five more odd and five more even numbers to the sets. Alternatively, they sort numbers in the range of 50 to 100 or 100 to 150.

Plenary

1, 2, 3, 4
Adjust the '1, 2, 3, 4' technique (p12). Children label themselves '1' to '3', and, on the roll of a dice, the child with the corresponding number reports for the group. If 4, 5 or 6 is thrown, roll the dice again.

Several groups present their statement about odd and even numbers.

Display all the groups' work informally and give children time to look at the work done by others.

(m) *So would 16 be odd or even? And 25?*

Why do you think this group chose to present their work in that way?

Assessment for learning

Can the children

(m) Recognise whether a number up to 30 is odd or even?

Tell their group which set they are going to put the next number in?

Label their work so that it is clear to others?

If not

(m) Make links with halving: use interlocking cubes to make a 'tower' representing numbers and see which towers break in half.

Make sure children are working at an appropriate level. Describe what they do and help them repeat the description.

Play 'Devil's advocate' (p11), showing a chart you have made which is incomprehensible because it lacks labels. Invite children to help you add labels to it.

Counting objects
Classroom technique: Talking partners

Using a context
Counting for counting's sake can be a dull task. A purpose, however, motivates children to count the coins, especially if it is an experience that they can relate to.

Estimation
Children's skills in estimation won't develop beyond guesswork unless practised regularly.

Strategies for counting
For example:
– Group and count the coins in tens (ensure children are confident to count in tens), then count the remainder.
– Group and count the coins in twos.
– Move aside each coin as it is counted.
– Pick up coins as they are counted and put them in a container.

Strategies
Encourage children to use different strategies to count the coins in each container.

Preparing for the plenary
As you observe the children, choose a pair with a useful counting strategy who can explain what they are doing to present their work in the plenary.

Introduction

Spread out forty-five 1p coins. Tell a story: a money jar fell on the floor and smashed open to reveal all these coins ... How much was saved?

Explain that it is useful to make an estimate before counting and that estimating is a way of checking: if the final number is totally different from the estimate, it may indicate an error has been made.

Children look carefully at the coins, then discuss an estimate with their partner.

Take feedback on the estimates and record them.

Begin to count the coins one at a time, but play 'Devil's advocate' (p11) and make deliberate errors: count some coins twice, forget to move counted coins aside so you lose your way, and so on. Ask children whether there is a better way to count the coins and invite pairs to demonstrate their strategies.

(m) *Which counting method would you use for a really large amount?*

(Speaking and listening icon) *Tell your partner whether the answer is close to your estimate.*

Pairs

Give each pair of children two containers filled with 1p coins or counters. Children explore which container they would most like to keep.

Ask pairs for a written estimate for each container before they start counting. Children write both their estimate and actual count on a sticky note and stick it to the relevant container. They check their actual count to make sure it was correct.

Allow about 5 minutes for estimating and counting, then ask pairs to swap tables. They check the amounts in the new containers and, if appropriate, edit the numbers on the sticky notes.

(Speaking and listening icon) *How do you say that amount as money?*

(Personal skills icon) *Will the next pair who counts those coins reach the same number as you?*

Support: Children work with less than 20 coins or counters.

Extend: Children use more than 100 coins or counters. Tell pairs that you expect efficient counting methods.

Plenary

Pairs return to their original table and look at the notes on the containers. Ask children to notice whether the other pair who counted the coins reached the same number.

One pair demonstrates to the class how they counted their coins.

Finally, children hold up the container they would like and tell their partner why they would like it.

(m) *Why is counting in tens a good idea?*

Did you and your partner work well together? If not, what could be changed?

Did the other pair agree with the number you and your partner had written on your containers? If they did, you must have counted well and checked your work – well done!

Assessment for learning

Can the children	**If not**
(m) Use an efficient strategy to count numbers of objects?	(m) Practise counting accurately in ones, emphasising one-to-one correspondence by moving, touching or reorganising the coins.
Speak clearly and look at their partner when talking to them?	Encourage children to make a game of whispering numbers, shouting them and speaking them clearly while looking at you or their partner.
Check their answers by recounting?	Put emphasis on checking work for a week or two, then revert to the idea of checking occasionally, reminding children of its value.

Name _____

Self and peer assessment

Lesson 1: Estimating	I think	My partner thinks
I can make estimates.		
I listen to my partner and repeat what they say.		

Lesson 2: Numbers to 100	I think	My partner thinks
I can count up to: _____		
I can ask and answer questions when we play the number game.		

Name _____

Self and peer assessment

Lesson 3: Odd and even numbers	I think	My partner thinks
(m) I know which numbers are odd and even.	🙂 ☹️	🙂 ☹️
I talk with my group about our work.	🙂 ☹️	🙂 ☹️

Lesson 4: Counting objects	I think	My partner thinks
(m) I can count lots of objects.	🙂 ☹️	🙂 ☹️
I talk with my partner about our work.	🙂 ☹️	🙂 ☹️

Place value and ordering

Learning objectives

	Lessons			
	5	6	7	8
ⓜ Maths objectives				
know what each digit represents in a two-digit number	●			
read and write whole numbers to 100		●		
know what each digit represents in a three-digit number			●	
order whole numbers to 100				●
Ⓢ Speaking and listening skills				
listen and follow instructions accurately	●			
listen with sustained concentration		●		
reach a common understanding with a partner			●	
listen to others and ask relevant questions				●
Ⓟ Personal skills				
work with others: work cooperatively with others	●			
work with others: overcome difficulties and recover from mistakes		●		
improve learning and performance: reflect on learning			●	
organise work: check work				●

About these lessons

Lesson 5: Representing numbers

 Know what each digit represents in a two-digit number

Equipment such as base-ten blocks and bundles of ten straws can help children develop a feel for the value of the digits in a two-digit number. This, in turn, gives children a secure understanding of the size of numbers and where numbers fit in the number system.

Listen and follow instructions accurately

Classroom technique: Talking stick

This technique gives children the opportunity to speak and be listened to. The child holding the 'talking stick' chooses a number to be made and dictates the type of resource to make it with.

Work with others: work cooperatively with others

Children share a task and must work together in order to fulfil it. Knowing that they will have a turn to hold the 'talking stick' acts as an incentive to cooperate.

Lesson 6: Reading numbers

 Read and write whole numbers to 100

Our language does not have simple rules to help children identify which part of the number to write first: 'seventeen' and 'seventy' sound very similar, but are written with the 7 in different positions. This Bingo game gets children to focus on reading number words and on linking them with the same number in figures.

Listen with sustained concentration

Classroom technique: Peer tutoring

Children take turns to be the 'Caller', reading out loud numbers presented in figures and words and helping the others in their group to identify the same number on their Bingo boards. The children with Bingo boards must listen carefully to the Caller, as the numbers are presented orally and with no visual clues.

Work with others: overcome difficulties and recover from mistakes

The 'Callers' act as tutors, helping the others in their group and gently correcting any mistakes. The Caller has the advantage of having read the number from their own sheet, where each number is shown in words and in figures.

Lesson 7: Place values

 Know what each digit represents in a three-digit number

Understanding place value lies at the heart of our number system. In this lesson, children play a game placing digits in different positions in a three-digit number and saying their values.

Reach a common understanding with a partner

Classroom technique: Peer tutoring

Children sometimes make good teachers because they can remember images, resources, language or phrases that helped them understand a piece of mathematics. In this lesson, pairs work together informally in a tutor/pupil relationship, working towards a shared understanding.

Improve learning and performance: reflect on learning

In the plenary, children discuss what maths they have been learning or practising in playing the game.

Lesson 8: Ordering numbers

 Order whole numbers to 100

Once children can order a set of consecutive numbers, they need to practise ordering a set of non-consecutive numbers. In this lesson, children generate their own numbers to put in order, then write them in the correct position on a 100-grid.

Listen to others and ask relevant questions

Classroom technique: One between two

Pairs first order a set of numbers. One child then takes the role of 'Solver' and describes to the 'Recorder' where to position one of these numbers on a 100-grid. The Recorder must listen to the instructions and ask questions to clarify any misunderstandings. Pairs swap roles until all numbers are recorded.

Organise work: check work

Children check their work against a 100-grid. This helps develop the good habit of checking for and correcting errors.

Representing numbers

Classroom technique: Talking stick

Learning objectives

(m) Maths
Know what each digit represents in a two-digit number

Speaking and listening
'Listen and follow instructions'
Listen and follow instructions accurately

Personal skills
'Work well with others'
Work with others: work cooperatively with others

(w) Words and phrases
hundreds, tens, ones, base ten, digit, represent, worth, value, how many, check

(r) Resources
'talking sticks'
base-ten blocks
place value arrow cards
straws as singles, bundles of 10 and 100
large sheets of paper
wipe boards

Tell your partner
Children turn to their neighbour and say the number and the value of each of the digits.

Tell your partner
Use this technique (p10) again.

Resources
Each group needs enough resources of different kinds to represent numbers to 99. If necessary, rotate resources around the groups so that the child with the 'talking stick' has some choice. Encourage children to use a range of different resources.

Overseeing work
Remind the child with the 'talking stick' that they are responsible for ensuring that the number is accurately represented.

Introduction

Write up a two-digit number on the board and establish the value of the digits.

Break down the number into tens and ones and write these separately.

> 99: 90 and 9

Give the 'talking stick' to a child. They come to the board and write another two-digit number. Again, establish the value of the digits.

The child then breaks down their number as before and passes the talking stick to another child.

> 43: 40 and 3

(m) *How do we know that 43 has 4 tens in it and not 3 tens?*

(m) *Can you choose a number that is greater than the last one we had?*

Groups of three or four

Groups share a 'talking stick'. The child with the stick writes a two-digit number on a wipe board and reads it to the group. They also choose how the group represent that number, using base-ten blocks or place value arrow cards, and oversee this.

When the group have made the number, each member sketches the representation on paper and records the number.

Children swap the 'talking stick' and repeat the process.

Towards the end of the session, all groups work with the same number so that you have representations of it, using different resources.

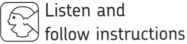
[m] *Have you got 56 straws there yet? How can you tell?*

[face] *When you had the 'talking stick', did the group listen well to your instructions?*

[smiley] *Have you worked well together? How?*

Support: Work with this group.

Extend: Work with three-digit numbers.

Plenary

Collect work from each group on the final, common number and display this informally for the class to look at. Children 'read' the number in these different representations and check they all show the same number.

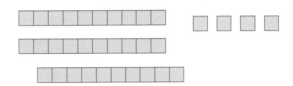

[m] *Can you count the straws in tens? 10, 20, 30, yes, and then 31, 32, 33, 34. There are 34 straws.*

[smiley] *We have worked as a class to show the number 34 in lots of different ways. Well done, class!*

Assessment for learning

Can the children

[m] Represent the place value of each digit in a number, using base-ten blocks? Bundles of straws? Sticks of cubes?

[face] Repeat what instructions they have been given by the child with the 'talking stick'?

[smiley] Share resources and tasks equally?

If not

[m] Do some work counting collections of objects and organising these into groups of 10.

[face] Ask the child with the 'talking stick' to repeat the instructions and help them check that all others have listened well and understood everything.

[smiley] Talk with the class about the meaning of working cooperatively with each other and focus on one good habit each time there is a group task.

Reading numbers

Classroom technique: Peer tutoring

Learning objectives

Maths
Read and write whole numbers to 100

Speaking and listening
'Listen well'
Listen with sustained concentration

Personal skills
'Get over difficulties and mistakes'
Work with others: overcome difficulties and recover from mistakes

Words and phrases
tens, ones, position, place value, worth, correct, error

Resources
display copy of RS3
boards cut from RS4
RS5
for each group:
boards cut from RS4
copy of RS5
counters
wipe boards
pens

Introduction

Display RS3 and read the numbers to 20 with the children.

Work with the class to create further two-digit numbers by combining elements from the first and last lists, writing the result on the board.

twenty-one   eighty-nine   forty-three

Play a class game of Bingo, with pairs of children sharing a board of ten numbers cut from RS4. Read out a number from RS5 and cross it out or cover it with a counter so you know you have used it. Children with that number (either as a numeral or written) cover it with a counter.

The first pairs to cover all their numbers win (several pairs will have the same board and so be joint winners). Continue until all pairs have finished.

(m) *How do we spell 'forty-four'? What do you notice about the spellings of the 'for' sound – is it the same in both parts of the word?*

(s) *I'll read the word just once. Agree with your partner what number I said.*

(p) *What order do the digits go in 31? Yes, a 3 and then a 1. If you got it the wrong way round, just put it right.*

Tell your partner
Orchestrate this: children listen to the number you say, then, in silence, look for it on their board. After a few seconds they turn to their partner and say whether they have that number.

Groups of four

Children play the game in groups of four. One child is the 'Caller', and the others each have a board from RS4. The Caller reads out a number from RS5 and checks with the other players, in turn, whether or not they have that number. If they do, the Caller gives out counters.

Groups play four games so that each child takes a turn to be Caller.

Peer tutoring
The 'Caller' acts as tutor, helping the other children in their group to spot the numbers called, gently correcting any mistakes. The Caller has the advantage of having read the number from their own sheet, where each number is shown in words and in figures.

 *Can you write 88 in words?*

 *What number did the Caller say?*

What letter does 'twenty-one' begin with? Does that help you check whether you have it on your board?

Support: The Caller works with another child who supports them in their role, but does not take over.

Extend: Four children each have a blank 2 × 5 grid and fill each square with a numeral or number word. Photocopy the four grids onto one master sheet so the group have the wherewithal to play Bingo.

Plenary

Work with a pair of children to create a two-digit number, as in the introduction, and write it up – but with several letters missing. The rest of the class, in pairs, write the word in full on their wipe boards. The pair fills in the missing letters and asks the class to correct their own work.

> s_xty- _ _ve

If you can spell 'seven', does that help you spell 'seventy'? Does spelling 'five' help you with 'fifty'?

How do you work out what letters are missing?

Assessment for learning

Can the children

Read 'fifty-eight', 'sixty-five', '97' and '44'?

Repeat the number that the 'Caller' has read out once?

Gracefully accept help from the Caller?

If not

Play the Bingo and missing-letters games regularly with children and make sure they are involved in creating number words (see Extend).

Practise listening skills with the class, using games such as 'Simon says', where children repeat what the leader has said, but only if this is preceded by the words 'Simon says'.

Talk with children about how learning at school is a group task and how, as in adult life, people can learn from, and also help, each other.

Place value

Classroom technique: Peer tutoring

Introduction

Display the number 111, using place value arrow cards, and ask the children to read it aloud.

Ask which of the three digits represents 'one ten', which 'one one' and which 'one hundred'. Pull the cards apart to reveal the value of the different digits.

To consolidate this understanding, work with the class to select the correct base-ten blocks and represent each part of 111.

(m) *Why is this 1 worth one hundred and this only worth one one?*

(s) *Tell your partner what number that would be if there was a 3 in the tens place.*

Groups of four

Groups of four children share two copies of RS6. Each child writes their name in one of the boxes under the heading 'Player's name'.

Children play a game, arranging numbers to form the highest possible number. Child A rolls the dice once and decides whether to write the number in the hundreds, tens or ones column. Once it is written in, Child A says the value of the digit – for example, "3 hundreds."

Children B, C and D repeat the above. They continue until everybody's three-digit number is complete. The player with the highest number is the winner and chooses which of the four numbers to make from base-ten blocks.

Children play up to four games on RS6, with a different child starting each game.

Peer tutoring
Observe children as they play and ask children who are competent with the task to support and tutor children who are not. If necessary, reorganise groupings.

Recording
Children record one of the three-digit numbers their group has created in their books and, alongside the number, draw what it looks like made from base-ten blocks.

Reach an understanding with your partner

(m) *What number have you made from the base-ten blocks?*

Tell your group how you know that this is the highest number.

Can you explain to Alaia what this digit means? Why is it worth a different amount in this column?

Support: Use RS7 showing tens and ones and provide a 0–100 number line for comparing numbers.

Extend: Use RS8 showing thousands, hundreds, tens and ones.

Plenary

Play the same game against the class, using only two rows of the grid on RS6. Take a vote to decide which position to place the class's digit in.

Briefly discuss what maths children have been learning or practising in this game: the different values a digit has when it is in different positions in a number.

Tell your neighbour where you think the 8 should go, and why.

Does drawing the number help you see why 3 in the hundreds column is different to 3 in the tens column?

What have you worked on today?

Devil's advocate
Using this technique (p11), occasionally say the incorrect value for digits or make a mistake when using base-ten equipment and ask children to correct your mistakes.

Assessment for learning

Can the children

(m) Correctly identify the value of the 5 in 45, 54 and 540?

Agree with their group who has made the highest number?

Name one or more things they have been learning or practising in the lesson?

If not

(m) Do further work making numbers with place value arrow cards and modelling them with base-ten blocks.

Ask children to play in pairs against another pair, discussing each move they make with their partner.

Make a point of specifying to children what they are learning in each lesson, or part of a lesson, so that they get used to thinking in these terms.

Ordering numbers

Classroom technique: One between two

Learning objectives

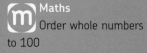
Maths
Order whole numbers to 100

Speaking and listening
'Listen to others and ask them questions'
Listen to others and ask relevant questions

Personal skills
'Check your work'
Organise work: check work

One between two
Introduce this technique (p8) which will be used in children's later independent work: Child A tells Child B where to write the number. The technique also models the kind of vocabulary children will need to use.

Words and phrases
highest/lowest, biggest/smallest, order, in between, above, below, column, row, position, correct, check

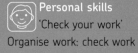
Resources
display copy of RS9
RS10
for each pair:
copy of RS9
0–9 dice
100-grids
wipe board
pens

One between two
Emphasise that pointing is not allowed. If necessary, ask the 'Solver' to sit on their hands. The 'Recorder' can ask further clarifying questions as to the positioning of the number.

Introduction

Display RS9 and write up these numbers:

61	74	80	73	72	68	75	69

Children discuss in pairs roughly where these numbers belong on a 100-grid.

Explain that the class need to put these numbers in order from smallest to largest.

Pairs share a wipe board and pen, decide which is the smallest number and record this. One pair says the smallest number, writes it in the correct place on RS9 and explains how they know its position.

All pairs write the remaining numbers in order on their wipe boards. Invite different pairs to the board to fill in the next number on the grid and to explain how they know this number is next in order, and where it should be positioned.

How do you know 74 is bigger than 70?

Do you mean 'write 73 in the threes column' or 'write 73 directly under the 3, near the number 11'?

Ask your partner which row to write 69 in.

Pairs

Pairs of children roll a 0–9 dice twice to generate a two-digit number and record it. They do this ten times to get ten numbers. Their first task is to work together to order them.

The pair then nominates a 'Solver' and a 'Recorder'. The Solver chooses a number to display and tells the Recorder where to write it on a shared copy of RS9.

Children swap roles after each number.

When the numbers have been ordered, children check their work, using a 100-grid, and correct any errors.

If you know where 71 is, how does that help you find 79?

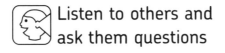

What can you ask your partner to be sure what she wants?

How can you check your work?

Are there any numbers that you need to change?

Support: Order fewer numbers, with a 100-grid for support if needed.

Extend: Children put a '1' in front of half of their numbers to turn them into three-digit numbers below 200, then position them on RS10.

Plenary

Display RS9 again. Children look at their own copies which will have ten extra numbers written in. Roll two 0–9 dice to generate a two-digit number. A pair of children explains to you where to write it in on the display grid, while the class also write the number on their own grids.

What number comes before 55?

Tell your partner whether you think they are writing 78 in the correct place.

Sharing work

Children take turns to write a number on the grid, while their partner checks their work.

Assessment for learning

Can the children	**If not**
Put in order 10 two-digit numbers?	Do similar work placing numbers to 30 or 50 on a partially filled-in number grid.
Repeat what their partner has just said about where a number belongs on the grid?	Do activities in which a child speaks to their partner, saying a number or the first few words of a rhyme, and their partner repeats back what was said.
Check the position of their numbers, using a 100-grid?	Have a 'checking week' in which children regularly check their own or their partner's work.

Self and peer assessment

Lesson 5: Representing numbers	I think	My partner thinks
(m) I can read the number 47 and say which is the tens digit and which is the ones digit.	☺ ☹	☺ ☹
I listen carefully to what other children say.	☺ ☹	☺ ☹

Lesson 6: Reading numbers	I think	My partner thinks
(m) I can read these numbers: sixty-five thirty-three ninety-one	☺ ☹	☺ ☹
I can say what number the 'Caller' has just said.	☺ ☹	☺ ☹

Name _____

Self and peer assessment

Lesson 7: Place value	I think	My partner thinks
(m) I know what the 3 means in the number 32.	🙂 ☹️	🙂 ☹️
I talk to the other children about the numbers we are making.	🙂 ☹️	🙂 ☹️

Lesson 8: Ordering numbers	I think	My partner thinks
(m) I can put numbers in order.	🙂 ☹️	🙂 ☹️
I listen when my partner talks about our work.	🙂 ☹️	🙂 ☹️

Calculations

Learning objectives

	Lessons			
	9	**10**	**11**	**12**
ⓜ Maths objectives				
calculate change	●			
solve mathematical problems		●		
recognise multiples in the 2 and 10 multiplication tables			●	
understand halving				●
🗩 Speaking and listening skills				
speak confidently in front of the class	●			
talk about shared work with a partner		●		
reach a common understanding with a partner			●	
contribute to whole-class discussion				●
🙂 Personal skills				
organise work: check work	●			
organise work: organise findings		●		
improve learning and performance: reflect on learning			●	●

About these lessons

Lesson 9: Shopkeeper's maths

 Calculate change

In this lesson, children practise 'shopping' within the context of a role-play scenario, which gives them the opportunity to come to terms with money, the various types of coin, calculating and giving change.

 Speak confidently in front of the class

Classroom technique: Tell the class

Children role-play shopper and shopkeeper in front of the class, modelling how they work out and give change.

 Organise work: check work

The child playing shopper checks that they are receiving the correct change before working with their partner to record the change on a resource sheet.

Lesson 10: Number bonds

 Solve mathematical problems

Children carry out and record an investigation about combinations, using five beans. They are introduced to the importance of working systematically.

 Talk about shared work with a partner

Classroom technique: Talking partners

The investigation should provoke informal discussion between pairs. Children, through the course of the activity, will need to reason, hypothesise and provide justifications for their answers.

 Organise work: organise findings

Children initially record their findings in their own way, but are then shown models of clear and systematic recording by their peers and, finally, by the teacher.

Lesson 11: Odd one out

 Recognise multiples in the 2 and 10 multiplication tables

Children need to know the number facts in the multiplication tables, and they also need to develop a feel for which tables numbers appear in. In this lesson, children work to identify what table a set of numbers belongs in and which number is the odd one out.

 Reach a common understanding with a partner

Classroom technique: 1, 2, 3, 4

When children share ideas or solutions with the class, the roll of a dice decides who will explain what they found out. Knowing that either partner may be called on to offer an explanation to the whole class encourages true sharing of ideas.

 Improve learning and performance: reflect on learning

In the plenary, children talk to their partners about the lesson and say what they think they have learned.

Lesson 12: Halving numbers

 Understand halving

Halving and doubling are key skills to support mental calculations. This lesson looks at ways to support the understanding of halving – a skill that children tend to use less than doubling.

 Contribute to whole-class discussion

Classroom technique: Talking partners

Children work together on a task and share ideas with their partner before committing themselves to offer ideas in a discussion with the whole class.

 Improve learning and performance: reflect on learning

An 'ideas map' is used in the introduction to establish what children already know about halving. This is then referred to during the plenary as a means to evaluate and record new learning.

Shopkeeper's maths
Classroom technique: Tell the class

Learning objectives

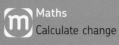 **Maths**
Calculate change

Speaking and listening
'Speak in front of the class'
Speak confidently in front of the class

Personal skills
'Check your work'
Organise work: check work

Words and phrases
count up, change, shopkeeper, pounds, pence, check, work out, answer

Resources
number line
display copy of RS13
RS12
for each pair:
copy of RS11 and RS13
coins
objects for a shop
and till
wipe boards

Staging the scene
Ensure the class are silent and listen to the dialogue. Ask the two children playing roles to pause every now and then while you ask questions to involve the class, using 'Tell the class' (p12).

Equivalence
Emphasise that the transaction is a fair one: the shopper hands over 50p, but gets back 50p's worth in goods and change. The layout of RS11 underlines the equivalence of the 50p coin handed over by the shopper and the toy and change handed over by the shopkeeper.

Checking
The shopper needs to check that they agree with the amount of change given by the shopkeeper.

Introduction

Set up a 'shop' in the home corner with books or toys, all priced below 50p, in multiples of 5p or 10p, and a till or box of coins holding 5p and 10p coins.

Children think through the process of buying something and receiving change. Collect in suggestions about relevant shopping vocabulary and write them up on the board.

> **Words we might use when we shop**
> change   coin   till   pence   pounds   money

Ask two confident children to role-play shopper and shopkeeper. The shopper has 50p, looks at the items on sale, chooses one to buy (stick to multiples of 10p at this stage) and makes the purchase. The shopkeeper receives the money and counts out the change.

Demonstrate clearly to the class the shopkeeper's procedure: handing over the item and stating its price, then counting up to the 50p in 5s or 10s while handing over the coins: "The toy is worth 20p. And this makes 30p ... 40p ... 50p." Model this on a number line marked in fives (see RS13).

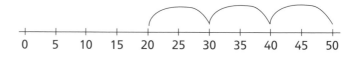

Repeat the change-giving process and number line modelling with other pairs and other shop items.

(m) *The book is worth 30p. And this makes 40p. Have I finished yet?*

(S) *How do you decide how much change to give?*

Pairs

Pairs act out the role-play scenario of shopper and shopkeeper. The shopkeeper is in charge of RS11. The shopper chooses a toy and places 50p on the picture of that toy. The shopkeeper works out the change to give, using a number line from RS13, then hands over the toy and the coins to the shopper.

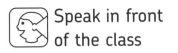
Both children work together to draw the coins on RS11 next to the toy.
After each transaction, children swap roles.

(m) *Show me how you find the change on the number line.*

(☺) *Why do you need to check your partner's answer?*

Support: Alter the prices so that toys cost multiples of 10p. Work with
children to model the transaction, using coins and real toys.

Extend: Use RS12, involving change from £1. Children can sketch empty
number lines.

Plenary

Different pairs role-play shopper and shopkeeper, either using calculations
they worked through on RS11 or making up their own problem. Stop the
proceedings just before the shopkeeper gives the change for the class to
check the shopkeeper's calculation, using a number line on RS13 or an
empty number line. Children write their answer on a wipe board and hold
it up for you.

(☺) *What does a shopper say? Can you say some words she might use?*

(☺) *How do you know the shopkeeper gave the correct change?*

Assessment for learning

Can the children	If not
(m) Find the change by counting up?	(m) Practise finding the difference between multiples of ten, using a number line to 'count up' from the lower to the higher number.
(☺) Role-play in front of the class?	(☺) Encourage children to act out the role-play scenario in a small group with children they feel confident having as partners.
(☺) Say why they need to check calculations?	(☺) Make some deliberate errors when doing calculations in front of the class. Ask children to help you check your work and give plenty of praise when they spot your errors.

Number bonds

Classroom technique: Talking partners

Learning objectives

(m) Maths
Solve mathematical problems

Speaking and listening
'Talk about your work with your partner'
Talk about shared work with a partner

Personal skills
'Organise your results'
Organise work: organise findings

(W) Words and phrases
pairs, altogether, add, plus, total, investigate, problem, record, solve, systematic

(r) Resources
for each pair:
five beans coloured red on one side and white on the reverse
paper plates (optional)

Introduction

Give each pair of children a paper plate and five bicoloured beans. Pairs take turns to toss the beans onto the plate and say the number of each colour they see.

> 3 red and 2 white

Observe pairs and ensure that both partners have a go at tossing the beans.

(m) *What is the total number of beans on the plate?*

(m) *If you had 5 red beans, how many white beans would there be?*

Pairs

Pairs of children investigate the different combinations of red and white that can be made with their five beans and find their own way of recording this.

After a few minutes, stop the class for a mini-plenary.

Give children more time to complete their investigation or to tidy up their recording. Children then tell you how many different combinations they think there are, showing the number by holding up their fingers.

Build on the children's own recording methods to show the different combinations on the board, working systematically. Include a record of the numbers involved.

What children may do

Children may start by tossing the beans and recording what happens (drawing and colouring the beans or making some kind of list). This will result in repeats, which children may, or may not, record. Some children may realise that they can investigate the problem systematically, without actually tossing the beans.

Repeats

This is an opportunity to address issues such as repeats and methods of recording. A few children briefly talk about their work and show their recording so far.

Solution

Regardless of how many beans there are, the number of combinations is always one plus the number of beans. The way the beans land on the plate is one combination; then you can turn over each bean once.

U&A Systematic recording

The more you model ways of systematic recording to the class, the richer the repertoire they can call on in future when doing work such as this.

	white	red
○○○○○	5	0
○○○○●	4	1
○○○●●	3	2
○○●●●	2	3
○●●●●	1	4
●●●●●	0	5

(icon) Talk about your work
with your partner

(m) *How many different pairs did you find?*

(icon) *How did you two share the work?*

(icon) *Could you show your results systematically?*

Support: Help children organise their recording so that they can recognise repeats and exclude them.

Extend: Children explore what happens with six beans and find all the ways to make 10 by adding two numbers. (This has similarities with the beans problem, although that may not be apparent to children.)

Plenary

Ticket to explain
Use this technique (p12).

Display the recording of the beans problem. Give pairs a few minutes to learn by heart the pairs of numbers that made up five beans, then hide the recording.

Pass a 'talking stick' around the class: the first child who holds it says two numbers that total 5, the next repeats that combination, then says their own, and so on. Expect many repetitions.

(m) *Four and what makes five?*

(m) *Is there a pair of numbers that nobody has said yet?*

Assessment for learning

Can the children	**If not**
(m) Find a way to answer your initial question?	(m) Work on more simple problems with the children, supporting them to record their work coherently.
(icon) Talk about what part they played in the shared work?	(icon) Prompt children with gentle questioning to help them understand and express their role in the work.
(icon) Organise their work to show the six combinations, recognising any repeats?	(icon) Take every opportunity to demonstrate the patterns underlying number so that children start to see numbers as organised rather than chaotic.

Odd one out

Classroom technique: 1, 2, 3, 4

Learning objectives

Maths
Recognise multiples in the 2 and 10 multiplication tables

Speaking and listening
'Reach an understanding with your partner'
Reach a common understanding with a partner

Personal skills
'Think about what you have learned'
Improve learning and performance: reflect on learning

Words and phrases
multiple, multiply, table, odd, even, set, odd one out, same, different, sort

Resources
display copy of RS14 and RS15
wipe boards
dice and dice labelled 1 and 2 only
labels with numbers 1 to 4 written on for each pair:
wipe boards
pens

Answers
The bottom part of RS14 has the answers – keep this hidden from view.

1, 2
Adjust the '1, 2, 3, 4' technique (p12). Pairs label themselves '1' or '2'. Roll a dice labelled with 1 and 2: if 2 comes up, the child with that number answers the question. This encourages both children to take responsibility for knowing and understanding the answer.

Odd one out
18 7 20 8
Accept answers such as:
"18, 20 and 8 are in the 2 multiplication table, but 7 isn't."

Introduction

Display the top left-hand part of RS14 and the multiplication grid on RS15. Read out the first set of four numbers (50, 100, 10 and 40). Children think about which multiplication table these numbers are from, then discuss it with their partner. Pairs record their answer on a wipe board and hold it up to you.

Confirm the children's answers by reference to the 100-grid and colour in the multiples of 10.

Go through the rest of the list in the same way, sometimes with the 100-grid hidden to encourage mental working.

Display the top right-hand part of RS14 with sets of four numbers, where three belong in the same table and one is the odd one out. Pairs work together to identify both the table and the number that does not fit and explain how they know this. Collect in suggestions from the class.

m *What can you say about numbers in the 2 times table?*

speaking *Explain to your partner how you can tell which number is the odd one out.*

Pairs

Pairs of children produce five sets of multiples from the 2 and 10 multiplication tables. Each set has four numbers, one of which is an odd one out. Children take turns with their partner to solve the problems, then swap papers with another pair.

m *How did you work out which table these numbers were in?*

m *Tell me a number in the 10 times table.*

speaking *What is the same about those numbers?*

Support: Help children model the numbers in the 2 times table by making towers from cubes or drawing jumps of two on a number line. They then list all the multiples and use these to make sets of multiples of 2, with one odd one out.

Reach an understanding with your partner

lesson **11**

Extend: Include the 3 and 5 multiplication tables.

Plenary

Children explain how they identified the odd one out in the sets they were given.

Scribe what children say and establish how to identify a multiple of 10. Pairs present one multiple of 10 on a wipe board.

Scribe several of the answers given, picking up on any misconceptions.

Multiple of 10:	Not a multiple of 10:
in a line on the 100-grid	in other places on the 100-grid
10 20 30	might end in 5 or 7
ends in 0	
Examples:	Examples:
50 60 90	45 67 96
30 100 200	23 11

Repeat this with the 2 times table.

Finish with reflecting on the lesson. Children take a moment to think alone, then tell their partner one thing they enjoyed doing in the lesson and one thing they have learned.

(m) *Is 25 really a multiple of 10?*

(☺) *Will you be quick at spotting a multiple of 10 in future?*

Assessment for learning

Can the children

(m) Recognise whether a number appears in the 2 or 10 multiplication table?

(☺) Explain what they and their partner have decided?

(☺) Say one thing they enjoyed about the lesson?

If not

(m) Practise counting in equal jumps from 0, sometimes making a deliberate mistake for children to spot.

(☺) Ask a child to give an explanation for their partner to repeat.

(☺) Offer suggestions for the child to agree or disagree with.

Halving numbers

Classroom technique: Talking partners

Learning objectives

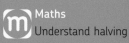

Maths
Understand halving

Speaking and listening
'Join in a discussion with the whole class'
Contribute to whole-class discussion

Personal skills
'Think about what you have learned'
Improve learning and performance: reflect on learning

Words and phrases
one whole, equal, halve, half, fraction, explain, reason, generalise

Resources
linking cubes
display calculator (optional)
large sheet of paper
for each pair:
copy of RS16

Halving odd numbers
All numbers can be halved (for example, half of 19 is $9\frac{1}{2}$), but the focus here is on halving to create two equal whole numbers.

Tell your partner
Give children a moment or two to check their halving before turning to their neighbour to describe what they have done.

Ideas map
Don't expect children of this age to be able to sort or organise the ideas on the map, but do so yourself, explaining your reasoning and drawing out linked vocabulary or ideas: "This sounds like the same kind of idea as that one, so I'll write it underneath." Illustrate some of the contributions.

Checking answers
Remind children to check each other's work: the child who made the stick knows its number of cubes, and whether it can be halved, and checks that their partner recorded these facts correctly.

Introduction

Provide each child with linking cubes. Children make a stick, break it in half if they can and reflect on what they have done.

Create an 'ideas map' either on the board or on a large sheet of paper pinned up in view of the class. Ask children what they know about halving and scribe all contributions even if they are repeated. Do not get drawn into dealing with misconceptions yet.

> Halves are the same.
>
> Numbers you can halve are even.
>
> My stick had 7 cubes, and it didn't break in half.
>
> They are in the 2 times table.
>
> You can halve 2.
>
> Half of 10 is 5.
>
> This is my stick in halves.

Encourage children, even if they do not contribute, to listen and think about all the points on the board.

ⓜ *Tell me some numbers that you can halve. What do they have in common?*

ⓜ *What does 'half' mean?*

🗪 *Can you add anything to the ideas map?*

Pairs

Pairs of children sit back to back. Each child makes a stick from cubes, counts the cubes and checks whether or not the stick breaks in half. They then turn to their partner and swap sticks. Their partner must predict out loud whether the stick they have been given will form two equal halves and check by breaking it.

Children write their own information on a shared copy of RS17.

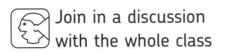

(m) *You found half of that number. What happens when you double that half?*

(☺) *Which numbers are easy for you to halve?*

Support: Work with sticks of no more than 12 cubes.

Extend: Children generalise about which numbers break in half, and which do not, and offer predictions for any number to 100.

Plenary

Children talk about which kinds of numbers break in half. Add their ideas to the ideas map and encourage discussion about these contributions.

> If you jump in twos, it's those numbers that break in half.

Links with division
Encourage children to tell you the calculator keys to press. This will help them see that to halve a number, you divide it by 2.

Ask for some examples of numbers that will, and some that won't, break in half and check these on a display calculator.

Finally, give children some thinking time to reflect on the lesson. Read out the ideas mapped so far and invite final suggestions for new ideas to add to it.

(m) *What buttons do I press to find half of 23?*

(☺) *Do you agree with what Toby just said? Why not?*

(☺) *Which of these ideas do you understand?*

Assessment for learning

Can the children

(m) Recognise which numbers can be halved to produce whole numbers and which cannot be halved?

(☺) Contribute an idea, a comment or an explanation to class discussion?

(☺) Identify an idea on the 'ideas map' they do understand?

If not

(m) Model halving in a variety of ways – with sticks of cubes, folding number lines in half, halving on a calculator – and make links with doubling.

(☺) Note which children do not speak and encourage them to join in class discussion on other occasions. Use a 'talking stick' to formalise the role of 'Speaker' and 'Listeners'.

(☺) Provide more opportunities for self-reflection in the plenary or as part of marking children's own work.

Name _____

Self and peer assessment

Lesson 9: Shopkeeper's maths	I think	My partner thinks
(m) I can pretend to be a shopkeeper and give the correct change.	🙂 ☹️	🙂 ☹️
I am brave enough to speak in front of the class.	🙂 ☹️	🙂 ☹️

Lesson 10: Number bonds	I think	My partner thinks
(m) I can solve problems.	🙂 ☹️	🙂 ☹️
I talk to my partner about our work.	🙂 ☹️	🙂 ☹️

Name _____

Self and peer assessment

Lesson 11: Odd one out	I think	My partner thinks
(m) I know what numbers are in the 2 and 10 times tables.	🙂 ☹️	🙂 ☹️
I talk with my partner about our work.	🙂 ☹️	🙂 ☹️

Lesson 12: Halving numbers	I think	My partner thinks
(m) I can find out whether a number can be halved.	🙂 ☹️	🙂 ☹️
I say something to the class when we are having a discussion.	🙂 ☹️	🙂 ☹️

Handling data

Learning objectives

	Lessons			
	13	**14**	**15**	**16**
Ⓜ Maths objectives				
sort and organise data	●			
organise information on a block graph and on a table		●		
solve a problem by organising information			●	
interpret block graphs				●
Ⓢ Speaking and listening skills				
explain and justify thinking	●			
talk about shared work with a partner		●		
contribute to small-group discussion			●	
reach a common understanding with a partner				●
Ⓟ Personal skills				
improve learning and performance: take pride in work	●			
organise work: check work		●		
organise work: organise findings			●	
improve learning and performance: develop confidence in own judgements				●

About these lessons

Lesson 13: Sorting cards

 Sort and organise data

In this lesson, children decide how to sort a pile of greetings cards by one consistent criterion. The fact that other children sort the same images in different ways underlines the idea that there is no correct or incorrect way to sort a set of objects.

 Explain and justify thinking

Classroom technique: Tell your partner

Children discuss their ideas with a partner before offering them to the class. Explaining the thinking behind children's ideas helps develop a class culture, where reason is valued and ideas can be checked or challenged.

 Improve learning and performance: take pride in work

Children work with attractive materials and know their work will go on display, so are encouraged to take care with the finished product.

Lesson 14: Block graph

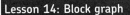

 Organise information on a block graph and on a table

Children analyse the parts of a graph and reproduce the findings on a table. They then use the table to reconstruct the graph and compare the two to check for discrepancies.

 Talk about shared work with a partner

Classroom technique: Eyes closed, eyes open

This technique is used in two different ways in this lesson: first, children listen carefully in order to count cubes dropped into a pot; then they look carefully to identify a change made to a graph while their eyes were closed. In both cases, they discuss their conclusions with their partner.

 Organise work: check work

Children have to keep comparing the graph they are making with the table showing the data to ensure the two show the same information. They then check a graph where some of the data has been changed to spot that change.

Lesson 15: Organising information

 Solve a problem by organising information

A key part of the data-handling cycle is ensuring that the question posed gets answered and recognising when this has happened. In this lesson, children are asked a simple question, but must decide how to organise the given data in order to answer that question.

 Contribute to small-group discussion

Classroom technique: Devil's advocate

Children work to organise data on a simple chart or table, then discuss statements (true, false or uncertain) about the data. Because children themselves have been active in collating the data, they are in a good position to discuss and agree the answers.

 Organise work: organise findings

Children practise their organisational skills, turning a simple list into a table or chart according to the number of letters in children's names.

Lesson 16: Interpreting graphs

 Interpret block graphs

The most important and useful part of the data-handling cycle is that of interpreting a chart. In this lesson, children are presented with a bar chart which is completed except for the labelling. This requires children to think hard about the meaning of what is shown in order to place labels in positions that make good sense overall.

 Reach a common understanding with a partner

Classroom technique: Talking partners

Pairs work as a team, discussing their ideas and sharing decision making to complete the given task.

Improve learning and performance: develop confidence in own judgements

Children are asked to think about which of the questions they have answered they feel most certain about. The purpose of this is to encourage children to notice their own level of confidence – or lack of it.

Sorting cards
Classroom technique: Tell your partner

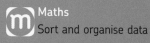
Introduction

Look with the children at a set of cards cut from RS18 and explain that these are the fronts of greetings cards. Set a context for sorting the images: there is a card shop, and the owner wants to display some of these cards grouped in similar sets in the shop window.

Children talk with their neighbour about a criterion for sorting the cards for a few minutes. Collect in suggestions from the class and scribe these:

> the ones with trees
>
> cards with circles on
>
> cards with three shapes
>
> triangles

One consistent criterion
Take this opportunity to talk about having just one criterion, which should be applied consistently. So 'trees and stars' is not acceptable, but 'plants' or 'growing things' is.

Choose a criterion and work with the children to sort the cards into cards with this property and those without. Establish what each set has in common and label them.

U&A Working systematically
Children look at each card in turn and decide which set it belongs in.

with circles	no circles

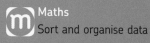 *What do all these cards have in common?*

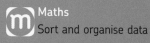 *If we sorted the cards in the way you suggest, how many would be in the set?*

Why do you think there aren't many cards that are the same?

Pairs

Take pride in work
Point out to the children that their work will go on display and that they need to take care with it.

Pairs of children share a set of cards cut from RS17. They discuss a way of sorting them by one criterion and carry this out.

Hold a mini-plenary in which you explore how children are sorting their cards and add any new criteria to the list on the board.

Children re-sort the images in sets and label these.

Which set has more cards? Could you find a way of sorting so there are more cards in this set than in the other one?

Tell me why that card belongs there.

What would be a really good way to sort the cards for the work you stick down and put on display?

Support: Help children choose a criterion for sorting the cards and remind them to look at each card before assigning it to a set.

Extend: Children find a way of sorting which puts roughly half the cards in each set.

Explain thinking

Children may find it difficult to explain the reasons behind their suggestions, but encourage them to try to do so. You want to encourage a class culture where opinions have reasons behind them that can be checked or challenged.

Playing again

This game, which can be played with many different materials, is intellectually challenging. Leave the cards out for children to play again in their own time.

Plenary

Play a game with the children. Divide a large sheet of paper in half and label the halves 'yes' and 'no'. Choose a criterion in secret and slowly start sorting the cards accordingly. Pause for children to discuss with their partner what they think the criterion might be and take a few suggestions and reasons for these.

If anyone guesses right, get the class to help you complete your sorting. Otherwise, continue and give children another chance to discuss with their partner.

Play several such games and invite children to help you choose the secret criterion.

Display children's work so the class can view all the sortings.

Who has chosen 'shape' to sort the cards by?

How do you know my criterion was 'overlapping shapes'?

Assessment for learning

Can the children

Sort the cards consistently by one criterion?

Explain why a card belongs in one set and not the other?

Say what they have done that they are pleased with?

If not

Model consistent sorting in class sessions, using children, numbers, shapes or toys.

Offer an explanation yourself and ask the child whether they agree and, if so, to repeat it back to you.

See if a child's partner can offer a suggestion that the child can agree with.

Block graph
Classroom technique: Eyes closed, eyes open

Learning objectives

(m) Maths
Organise information on
a block graph and on a table

Speaking and listening
'Talk about your work
with your partner'
Talk about shared work with
a partner

Personal skills
'Check your work'
Organise work: check work

(w) Words and phrases
count, record, collect,
most/least popular, block
graph, table, analyse, check

(r) Resources
graph made from
linking cubes prepared
in advance
metal pot or dish
for each pair:
linking cubes or
squared paper
pens

Eyes closed, eyes open
Children must listen carefully
to count the cubes accurately.

One between two
This would be a good
opportunity for children to
practise this technique (p8).

Recording
Remind children to give their
graph an axis label and a title.

Introduction
Present a block graph made from linking cubes.

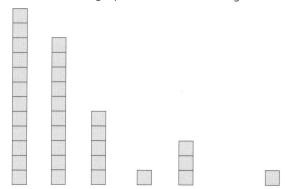

Red   Blue   Yellow   White   Purple   Black   Brown

Explain that the graph represents data collected from
a class in another school. The children were asked for
their favourite colour, and each stick represents the
children who chose that colour.

Ask the class to close their eyes, then break up each
stick, in turn. Children count as you drop the blocks
into a metal pot. After each stick is counted, children
open their eyes and check the number with their
neighbour. The class then help you record the blocks on
a table, remembering to label the table and columns.

Favourite colours in Class X

Colour	Number of children
Red	12
Blue	10
Yellow	5
White	1
Purple	3
Black	0
Brown	1

(m) *What do I need to write next on the table?*
Where shall I write it?

(m) *Is the table complete yet?*

(☺) *How can we check that there really were
5 yellow cubes?*

Pairs
Pairs of children use linking cubes or squared paper to
recreate the block graph, extracting the information
from the table.

Talk about your work with your partner

(m) *Do you prefer the table or the graph? Which is easier to get information from?*

Were there no people who chose black? Tell your partner why you think that.

Does the graph show the same information as the table?

Support: Children work with linking cubes.

Extend: Children work with squared paper.

Plenary

Eyes closed, eyes open again
Earlier, children closed their eyes to focus on listening. Here, the purpose is to keep hidden from children a change you have made, which they must then identify and describe.

Chewing the fat
Leaving questions unresolved provides thoughtful children with the opportunity to take away a problem to think over in private.

Leave on display the table created in the introduction. Display one of the children's graphs made from linking cubes. Children close their eyes while you change one element of the graph (remove a cube, add a cube, remove or swap a label).

Pairs discuss what has been changed, referring to the table as necessary. Ask for instructions as to how to restore the graph so it matches the table.

Finally, children think about whether the data on favourite colours used in this lesson would be the same as their own class.

(m) *Which part of the block graph does not match the table?*

Check that the graph and table now match, because I might have changed more than one thing.

Assessment for learning

Can the children

(m) Spot a discrepancy between the graph and the table?

Listen to and repeat what their partner says?

Spontaneously check that their graph matches the table?

If not

(m) Identify a real or false discrepancy yourself and ask the child to check whether or not the data matches.

Practise listening skills with the class, using games such as 'Simon says', where children repeat what the leader has said, but only if this is preceded by the words 'Simon says'.

Have a blitz on checking work when it is finished before handing it in. Ask children to remind each other about checking their work.

Organising information

Classroom technique: Devil's advocate

Learning objectives

Maths
Solve a problem by organising information

Speaking and listening
'Join in a discussion with a small group'
Contribute to small-group discussion

Personal skills
'Organise your results'
Organise work: organise findings

Words and phrases
count, record, collect, most/least, popular, table, tally, statement, true, false, reason, explain

Resources
for each group: alphabetical list of the names of children in the class

A meaningful context
Children have a natural interest in themselves and their peers, which you can use to involve them in a simple investigation.

Discuss and agree ways of working
As well as organising their findings, children will be addressing another personal skill: discussing and agreeing ways of working with others. The task is left open, so you must judge how much to intervene in groups' arrangements and how much you trust them to organise the task themselves.

Introduction

Pose the question: "Is it true that most children in this class have names with four letters?" Write up a few first names of children as a sample (choose various name lengths). Children discuss in groups of three what they think the answer will be.

Faran	Jack	Debbie	Ben	Harrison

Collect in a few suggestions, but make no comment on these.

Tell your group how we could find out the answer.

Groups of three

Each group has an alphabetical list of the names of children in the class and decides on a strategy for answering the question, then carries it out.

Stop the class after a few minutes for a mini-plenary. Groups explain how they are tackling the task and check whether they are happy with their chosen method or would prefer to change to a different one.

At the end, groups record their answer, compare their results with another group and check that these tally.

Did both of your groups solve a problem in the same way?

What do you think you need to do next? Do the rest of you agree?

Will anyone else know what that mark means if they look at your chart?

Support: Provide a predrawn table for children to complete.

Extend: Groups write some true and false statements about the data, which you can use in the plenary.

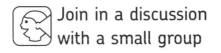
Plenary

Sketch your own table on the board, taking data from the groups.

Letters in name	Number of children
2 letters	0
3 letters	2
4 letters	5
5 letters	6
6 letters	9
7 letters	5
8 letters	2

Statements

For example:

There are six children with five-letter names.

Nobody has three letters in their name.

One child has a nine-letter name.

Quickly agree the answer to your original question. Then make some true, false and uncertain statements about the data for the groups to discuss.

Children give reasons for their answers.

Why can't we answer that question? Could we find out the answer at all?

Is there any other way of showing this information?

Is there an even quicker way of showing this information?

Assessment for learning

Can the children

Find a way to answer the original question?

Listen to what another group member has to say, without interrupting?

Record the data in such a way that it makes sense to others?

If not

Organise groups for similar work, where the child is supported by competent achievers, and ask them to act as peer tutors (p8).

Practise this skill with the class in pairs: each child talks for exactly one minute about a topic such as what they did at the weekend, while their partner listens.

Work with the child on activities such as the one in Lesson 16, where children need to put labels on a chart in order for it to make sense. Discuss with them what the chart means and what conclusions can be drawn from it.

Interpreting graphs
Classroom technique: Talking partners

Learning objectives

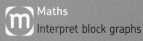

Maths
Interpret block graphs

Speaking and listening
'Reach an understanding with your partner'
Reach a common understanding with a partner

Personal skills
'Develop confidence about what you think and decide'
Improve learning and performance: develop confidence in own judgements

Words and phrases
count, record, most/least often, block graph, analyse, check, question, evidence, reason

Resources
sticky notes
for each pair:
copy of RS18
wipe boards

Introduction

Introduce a fictitious school, Bellfield School, with a headteacher called Mr Jones. Draw two axes on the board. Write 'Number of vehicles' next to the vertical axis and display columns of blocks (sketched or made from sticky notes) above the horizontal axis. Explain that the chart shows data about traffic seen on the road outside Bellfield School early one morning.

Write up these types of transport: 'car', 'lorry', 'milk float', 'bus' and 'bicycle'. Children discuss with their neighbour which label they would place where under the horizontal axis, and why.

Talking partners
Children turn to their partner and discuss this for a minute or two. Give them time to think about it, then take suggestions from the class. Emphasise that there is no correct answer, just ideas and reasons.

Traffic seen on the road outside Bellfield School early one morning

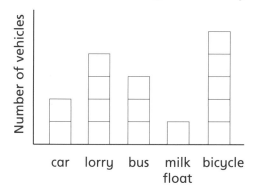

(m) *Why do you think we could put 'lorry' here?*

(m) *What time was the survey carried out? What vehicles might be around then?*

(m) *How many vehicles were recorded in the survey?*

(s) *Discuss with your partner if you would get the same results at 4 pm.*

Pairs

Pairs of children share a copy of RS18 to complete. Explain that the graph is fictitious, but that you want it to look plausible, so children need to think carefully about what vehicles to write in which column.

Pairs also invent three questions about their graph.

Children's questions
For example:
How many cars did Mr Jones travel in when on holiday?
Did more cars or vans park in the school yesterday?
Did any tractors go along the road?

Reach an understanding with your partner

Pairs then swap charts and questions with another
pair, using the chart they have been given to answer the questions.

(m) *Tell me about your graph ... And what else?*

(☺) *Do you agree with what your partner said? Why/Why not?*

(☺) *You seem certain about that answer. Tell me why.*

Support: Help children write the title and types of transport on their chart
and have an adult scribe their questions.

Extend: Children construct a story explaining their chart: "Yesterday, there
was a fire at Bellfield School, and seven fire engines came ..."

Plenary

A pair of children reads out one question they had to answer, which they feel
sure about, and shows the class the relevant chart. The rest of the class look
at the chart and write an answer on wipe boards. The pair acts as teacher,
asking the class to hold up their boards and confirming the correct answer.

(☺) *What would we need to change about this graph so that there were the
same number of vans and buses?*

(☺) *Explain how you know the answer to that question.*

Assessment for learning

Can the children

(m) Answer one or more questions about a graph,
posed by other children?

(☺) Identify something that they and their partner
agree about?

(☺) Choose a question they feel confident about
answering?

If not

(m) Make and discuss 'real' graphs, using transport
pictures or toy vehicles.

(☺) Ask children to say something themselves about
their work and see if their partner agrees with
the statement.

(☺) Ask some simple questions and encourage children
to answer those in confident tones. Consider
whether they would benefit from working at a
slightly less challenging level for a while to build up
their self-confidence.

Name _____

Self and peer assessment

Lesson 13: Sorting cards	I think	My partner thinks
(m) I can choose different ways to sort a collection of pictures.	😊 ☹️	😊 ☹️
I can explain why a card goes in a particular set.	😊 ☹️	😊 ☹️

Lesson 14: Block graph	I think	My partner thinks
(m) I can make an accurate graph.	😊 ☹️	😊 ☹️
I listen to what my partner says.	😊 ☹️	😊 ☹️

Name _____

Lesson 15: Organising information	I think	My partner thinks
(m) I managed to solve the problem about children's names.	☺ ☹	☺ ☹
(face icon) I listen when children in my group are talking.	☺ ☹	☺ ☹

Lesson 16: Interpreting graphs	I think	My partner thinks
(m) I can make sense of block graphs.	☺ ☹	☺ ☹
(face icon) I talk with my partner about our work.	☺ ☹	☺ ☹

75

Handling data

Self and peer assessment

Measures

Learning objectives

	Lessons			
	17	**18**	**19**	**20**
ⓜ Maths objectives				
estimate, measure and compare lengths	●	●		
know significant times in the year			●	
suggest suitable units to measure capacity, length and weight				●
Speaking and listening skills				
give accurate instructions	●			
talk about shared work with a partner		●		
speak confidently in front of the class			●	
contribute to small-group discussion				●
Personal skills				
work with others: show awareness and understanding of others' needs	●			
organise work: identify stages in the process of fulfilling a task		●		
improve learning and performance: take pride in work			●	
improve learning and performance: develop confidence in own judgements				●

About these lessons

Lesson 17: Working with lengths 1

 Estimate, measure and compare lengths

To solve a problem involving making a set of nesting loops (cylinders), children need to measure and/or compare the lengths of strips of card. For half the class, the mathematics is reinforced by explaining the task to other children and supporting them as they carry it out.

 Give accurate instructions

Classroom technique: Peer tutoring

Half the class make three nesting loops (cylinders) from strips of card. They then join up with a pair of children who have not done this task and act as peer tutors, explaining the task and supporting the pair in making their own set of nesting loops.

 Work with others: show awareness and understanding of others' needs

Children in the role of tutors need to be sensitive to their pupils' needs. They should allow their pupils to make their own decisions, but be available to help them as needed.

Lesson 18: Working with lengths 2

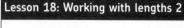 **Estimate, measure and compare lengths**

The lesson uses the fantasy context of giants, but draws on a child's personal experience of everyday objects: a knife, fork and spoon. Children solve a problem involving comparing and measuring the lengths of the giant's cutlery to help the giant replace her lost pieces.

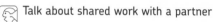 **Talk about shared work with a partner**

Classroom technique: Talking partners

The problem should provoke informal discussion between pairs as children discuss what to do, how to estimate or measure and how to overcome any difficulties they encounter in the process.

 Organise work: identify stages in the process of fulfilling a task

Pairs need to keep track of what they have done and what they still need to do. They are supported in this by the sense of purpose given by the fantasy context of the giant they are helping.

Lesson 19: Calendar

 Know significant times in the year

Calendars model the passing of days and the regular weekly cycle in an organised way that can help children structure their own sense of time. This lesson helps children understand this regular pattern by making their own calendar for one month, supported by the skeleton calendar provided on a resource sheet.

 Speak confidently in front of the class

Classroom technique: Talking stick

Children talk about a significant date when they hold the 'talking stick'. This allows each child the opportunity to speak in front of the class and guarantees that they are being heard.

 Improve learning and performance: take pride in work

Constructing their own personal calendar is an opportunity to work carefully and to take pride in their achievement.

Lesson 20: Measuring units

 Suggest suitable units to measure capacity, length and weight

In this activity, children read statements about measurement units and decide whether or not they are true. This helps them develop a feel for units of measure, which is essential for adult life.

 Contribute to small-group discussion

Classroom technique: Think, pair, share

Children consider a problem individually, then explain their ideas to a partner. After the pairs have discussed the issue, they get together with another pair, share views and emerge with a group conclusion.

 Improve learning and performance: develop confidence in own judgements

Children focus on deciding whether a statement about a measurement unit sounds likely to be true. Thinking about and discussing these measurements can give children a better sense of size and help them feel confident about their decisions.

Working with lengths 1
Classroom technique: Peer tutoring

Learning objectives

(m) Maths
Estimate, measure and compare lengths

(😊) Speaking and listening
'Give instructions'
Give accurate instructions

(🙂) Personal skills
'Think about what other people need'
Work with others: show awareness and understanding of others' needs

(w) Words and phrases
cylinder, length, long, longer, shorter, centimetre, compare, measure, exact, ruler

(r) Resources
nesting objects or shapes (nesting boxes, Russian dolls, a dart board)
for each pair:
set of nesting objects or shapes
ruler
scissors
strips of card
glue or sticky tape

Organising the class
Children of all abilities should have the opportunity to act as peer tutors in this and similar activities. On another occasion, arrange an activity where children who were in the role of pupils act as tutors.

Acting as tutor
Tutors need to be sensitive to their pupils' needs. Hold a mini-plenary to discuss this and emphasise that the tutors are acting as a support and advisor – they should allow their pupils to make decisions, but help them as needed.

Introduction

Illustrate the concept of nesting objects or shapes by showing a set of boxes, Russian dolls or the rings on a dart board.

Circulate the objects among the class so that children can feel them and ask questions.

(m) *What is the same about these dolls? And what is different?*

(m) *What can you say about their heights? And the distance around their tummies?*

Pairs

Divide the class in half. Give one half a straightforward activity such as drawing the set of Russian dolls. The other half have a secret assignment, which the children who are drawing do not yet know about: they are to work in pairs to make three nesting loops (cylinders) from strips of card. Pairs share a ruler, scissors and tape and strips of card all the same length. Explain that the cylinders should glide in and out of each other, so there must be enough of a gap, but not too much, and the gaps between them should be roughly equal.

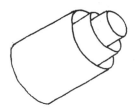

When a pair has completed the task, they get together with a pair of children who has not done this task and act as peer tutors, explaining the task and supporting the pair in making their own set of nesting loops.

Provide a table or shelf for children to display their work and remind them to write their names on it.

(m) *Does the length of the strip change when you bend it round? Why not?*

(icon) *Can you explain what you made?*

(icon) *Can you tell your pupils what lengths of card you used for your own loops?*

(icon) *What kind of help might your pupils need?*

Support: Direct children to cut strips of 30 cm, 20 cm and 10 cm. Children with fine-motor skills difficulties may need support to cut and use the tape.

Extend: Children make a set of four or five loops.

Plenary

Invite children to look at the work on display.

Finally, talk about the experience of tutoring and being tutored. Invite children to say one thing they liked or appreciated about the way their tutor helped them. Ask tutors what it felt like to be helping another child.

(m) *Are the nesting loops all the same heights?*

(icon) *Was it easy to know what help to give your pupils?*

Assessment for learning

Can the children

(m) Solve the problems by making strips of different lengths?

(icon) Describe the task accurately to their pupils?

(icon) Refrain from giving too much help to their pupils?

If not

(m) Work with children on making models from card and junk containers.

(icon) Make a point of explaining a task to the class for a few days, then asking them to redescribe it to their partner.

(icon) Ask the tutor to say nothing unless asked for help by their pupils. Give them their own simple drawing task to occupy them when they are not needed.

Working with lengths 2
Classroom technique: Talking partners

Learning objectives

Maths
Estimate, measure and compare lengths

Speaking and listening
'Talk about your work with your partner'
Talk about shared work with a partner

Personal skills
'Keep track of where you are'
Organise work: identify stages in the process of fulfilling a task

Words and phrases
length, width, longer, shorter, centimetre, same, different, estimate, measure, approximate

Resources
display copy of RS19
RS20
for each pair:
two copies of RS19 or RS20
set of plastic knife, fork and spoon
A4 card
scissors
glue
rulers and/or tape measures

Solving problems 1
Some children may well work by eye, rather than using rulers to measure, as they are developing a feel for estimation and proportion; however, if you want them to measure in centimetres, use RS20 instead of RS19.

Solving problems 2
Children will realise that the length of the knife needs to be longer than the sheet of card and the ruler. Observe the strategies children use to solve this problem – for example, do they join two sheets of card together, do they use a tape measure or a metre stick?

Introduction

Display RS19 and read out the giant's letter. Discuss the problem and look at some real cutlery. Establish that the giant's spoon needs to be roughly the same length as the fork, but the knife should be longer.

(m) *How tall do you think the giant is? Would she fit through the classroom door?*

(m) *Using your arms, can you show me the approximate length of the spoon?*

(m) *Is a real knife longer or shorter than a fork? How much?*

Pairs

Pairs of children work with two copies of RS19, drawing a knife and a spoon the correct size to send to the giant.

Observe pairs working, offering prompts for extending children's thinking as necessary: "Is the bowl of the spoon in proportion?"; "Are the handles wide enough?"

(m) *What length is the knife you have drawn?*

(s) *What does your partner think about what you just told me?*

(p) *What do you need to do next? And then?*

(p) *Have you finished yet? How will you know when you have finished?*

Support: Children work as peer tutors (p8), supporting less confident children. Make sure the tutors are working on the same table as the children needing support, so the relationship can be an informal one.

Extend: Children work with RS20, where the giant has given the length of the fork rather than a picture. They will need to measure lengths rather than work by eye.

Plenary

Provide a table or board for children to display their work and remind them to write their names on it.

Discuss the various responses to the giant's request, comparing and contrasting the results.

(m) *Are the knives all the same length? Which is the longest/shortest?*

(m) *Can you read the length Harry has written beside his spoon?*

Assessment for learning

Can the children

(m) Draw a spoon and knife of approximately suitable lengths and proportions?

Make a suggestion to their partner about what to do next?

Describe what they have done so far and what they still need to do?

If not

(m) Encourage children to look at the range of completed work and pick the ones they think 'look the right size'. Accept that a better sense of proportion will develop with greater maturity.

Make such a suggestion yourself and ask the child to repeat it.

Describe some of this yourself and ask the child to agree or disagree with what you have said. Make a point of talking with children about the progress of their work and what they still need to do to complete it.

Calendar
Classroom technique: Talking stick

Learning objectives

(m) Maths
Know significant times in the year

Speaking and listening
'Speak in front of the class'
Speak confidently in front of the class

Personal skills
'Take pride in your work'
Improve learning and performance: take pride in work

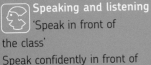 **Words and phrases**
day, date, month, year, week, January, February, ... December, calendar, record

(r) Resources
display copy of RS21
current calendar
for each pair:
two copies of RS21
coloured pens or pencils
talking stick

"Thirty days ..."
Recite the familiar rhyme with the children to help them work out how many days the month in question has.

Introduction

Have available a calendar of the month you want to work with. Display RS21 and establish what day of the week the first of the month falls on. Start to fill in the dates, but stop after about the 7th. Establish the last date in the month and write that in, too.

Month _____

Monday	Tuesday	Wednesday	Thursday	Friday	Saturday	Sunday
		1	2	3	4	5
6	7					

Talk with the children about any significant events and activities that will occur, or have occurred, during the month: outings, after-school clubs, days off, and so on. Record each event on the board as a simple list, with the day and/or date beside it.

Nature club	Wednesdays
Swimming	Tuesdays
Day off	21st February
Falconry visit	23rd February

(m) *How many days does February have?*

(m) *If February 1st is on a Wednesday, what will the date be on the Sunday after that?*

(S) *Can you say the rhyme about the months?*

Individuals/Pairs

Take pride in work
Encourage children to make a beautiful calendar that they can be proud of and take home to show their families.

Each child works with a copy of RS21. They write in all the dates, fairly small, and add words or pictures to show dates of significance to them. Children then work in pairs, sharing ideas and supporting each other, if necessary, and checking each other's work.

(m) *What day of the week does half-term start?*

(m) *What happens on Wednesdays this term? Will it happen on Wednesdays in half-term?*

Are you pleased with your calendar? How could you make it even more wonderful?

Support: Provide a real calendar for children to copy the dates from.

Extend: Children draw their own calendar on 2 cm squared paper.

Plenary

Pass around a 'talking stick'. The child with the stick holds up their calendar to show the class, reads out one key date and explains why that date is significant.

Tell us why January 29th is so important.

Which day of the week do you like best? Why is that?

Assessment for learning

Can the children	**If not**
(m) Write in the dates in order on their calendar?	(m) Ask children to work with a partner who can tell them what numbers to write where, perhaps using a real calendar as a guide.
Speak clearly and confidently in front of the class?	Ask children to whisper to you and relay the message for them. Set up small-group activities and games which require speaking in turn.
Produce work that they are proud of?	Point out the best things about children's work and remind them next time of what they have shown they are capable of.

Measuring units

Classroom technique: Think, pair, share

Learning objectives

Maths
Suggest suitable units to measure capacity, length and weight

Speaking and listening
'Join in a discussion with a small group'
Contribute to small-group discussion

Personal skills
'Develop confidence about what you think and decide'
Improve learning and performance: develop confidence in own judgements

Words and phrases
measure, size, capacity, length, height, weight, centimetre, metre, centimetres, kilogram, gram, litre, millilitre

Resources
display copy of RS22
for each pair:
copy of RS22
metre rule, ruler, litre measure
objects such as a litre carton of juice or a kilogram bag of sugar

---

Working with imagery
This will give children benchmarks as a basis for their imaginings and discussions.

U&A Reasoning
Tell children that you will be asking for reasons for their chosen answers.

Think, pair, share
The procedure is:
– individual considers questions
– pair shares thoughts
– two pairs join together and aim to reach consensus

Introduction

Display RS22 and read through the list of six true facts. In each case, help children construct a mental image of the object in question. Use a metre rule to work out how tall the woman is, ask children to imagine holding an apple in their hands, show children a litre jug or carton, and so on.

Revise the related equivalent measures and write these up for the class to refer to in the lesson.

> 1 metre = 100 centimetres
> 1 kilogram = 1000 grams
> 1 litre = 1000 millilitres

 Is 200 millilitres more or less than a litre? Why do you think that?

Does imagining a bag of sugar help you think about how much a kilogram is?

Pairs/Groups of four

Pairs share a copy of RS22. Read through the second set of facts with the class, without comment. Individuals read the statements again and think about them, then discuss with their partner whether each one is likely to be true or not, reaching agreement where possible.

Pairs then join with another pair and compare their ideas, aiming to reach agreement.

Think about the ruler which was 30 centimetres long. Would a tree be 20 centimetres?

What might weigh about one kilogram? Remember the sugar?

Explain to Raj why you think that must be false.

Check your answers and see if there are any you are unsure about. Ask the other pair about them.

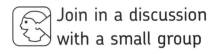
Support: Give this group the objects or tools you worked with in the introduction, such as a centimetre ruler, a kilogram of sugar, a litre of juice.

Extend: Pairs write their own 'facts' on the bottom of RS22 for their partner pair to tackle.

Plenary

Choose a group of four children. Read out one of the 'facts' and ask one of the group to answer it, giving their reasons.

Repeat with other groups and other questions.

Ⓜ *Do you think a book might weigh the same as 500 bags of sugar?*

☺ *You seem certain about that answer. Tell me why.*

Use 1, 2, 3, 4
Using this technique (p12), number the children 1, 2, 3 and 4. Roll a dice to determine which of them answers your question (roll again if you get 5 or 6).

Assessment for learning

Can the children

Ⓜ Make appropriate judgements about the 'facts'?

🗫 Take part in the discussion when pairs join up?

☺ Talk about when and why they are sure of an answer, and when not?

If not

Ⓜ Establish which measures and which particular units children have problems with and do further practical work on using these measures.

🗫 Consider introducing a 'talking stick' (p10) for group discussion.

☺ Work to create a classroom climate where uncertainty is accepted but where 'having a go' is also valued.

Name _____

Self and peer assessment

Lesson 17: Working with lengths 1	I think	My partner thinks
(m) I solved a problem about making nesting loops (cylinders).	☺ ☹	☺ ☹
I helped explain the task to my pupil.	☺ ☹	☺ ☹

Lesson 18: Working with lengths 2	I think	My partner thinks
(m) I successfully drew a knife and spoon for the giant.	☺ ☹	☺ ☹
I talk to my partner about our work.	☺ ☹	☺ ☹

Name _____

Lesson 19: Calendar	I think	My partner thinks
(m) I know how to use a calendar.	🙂 ☹️	🙂 ☹️
👤 I can speak in front of the class.	🙂 ☹️	🙂 ☹️

Lesson 20: Measuring units	I think	My partner thinks
(m) I am learning about measuring units.	🙂 ☹️	🙂 ☹️
👤 I join in the discussion with my group.	🙂 ☹️	🙂 ☹️

Self and peer assessment

Shape and space

Learning objectives

	Lessons			
	21	**22**	**23**	**24**
ⓜ Maths objectives				
use mathematical vocabulary to describe 2D shapes	●			
draw a simple map		●		
recognise line symmetry			●	
use mathematical names for common 2D shapes				●
Ⓢ Speaking and listening skills				
give accurate instructions	●			
reach a common understanding with a partner		●		
contribute to small-group discussion			●	
talk about shared work with a partner				●
Ⓟ Personal skills				
improve learning and performance: critically evaluate own work	●			
work with others: work cooperatively with others		●	●	
work with others: overcome difficulties and recover from mistakes				●

About these lessons

Lesson 21: Describing shapes

 Use mathematical vocabulary to describe 2D shapes

Children need to experience and talk about a wide range of shapes – not just squares, equilateral triangles and regular hexagons. This activity enourages children to look carefully at various shapes, thinking about and describing their properties.

 Give accurate instructions

Classroom technique: Barrier game

Children sit with their back to their partner. One child chooses a shape from the sheet, describes it and puts a counter on it. Their partner has a copy of the same sheet, but must rely on the verbal instructions to put a counter on the same shape on their sheet.

 Improve learning and performance: critically evaluate own work

In the plenary, children focus on the maths and speaking and listening objectives of the lesson, thinking about how they have achieved each objective.

Lesson 22: Drawing maps

 Draw a simple map

Children practise simple mapping skills, as they work together to construct a map showing a child in the playground and what is in front, behind, to the left and the right of them. This map focuses on direction, rather than accurately mapping distance.

 Reach a common understanding with a partner

Classroom technique: Talking partners

Children work informally together in a group of three, sharing and discussing a joint task.

 Work with others: work cooperatively with others

Children share decision making when producing a map, speaking and listening to each other and agreeing on how to proceed with the task.

Lesson 23: Using symmetry

 Recognise line symmetry

The activity consolidates children's understanding of symmetry through looking for pairs of shapes which can be combined to form one symmetrical shape. In discussing whether shapes form a pair, children use associated language.

 Contribute to small-group discussion

Classroom technique: Rotating roles

Children take turns to fulfil each of the three different roles in the group, thus ensuring that each of them participates fully. This paves the way for the discussion in which children prepare to present their ideas in the plenary.

 Work with others: work cooperatively with others

Although children have different roles, they all share the same task and must cooperate in order to complete it.

Lesson 24: Identifying shapes

 Use mathematical names for common 2D shapes

Children are shown two shapes, joined to disguise their true outlines. They try to work out what these shapes are, drawing on their knowledge of the properties and names of 2D shapes.

 Talk about shared work with a partner

Classroom technique: Tell your partner

Even though the teacher cannot take ideas and suggestions from everybody, the whole class can be involved and have a chance to speak, as each child turns to their partner and shares their ideas and solutions.

 Work with others: overcome difficulties and recover from mistakes

Children's willingness to persist with work they find hard can be encouraged by developing a classroom ethos of 'having a go' and by valuing effort as well as success. In this lesson, children are offered strategies to help them overcome difficulties.

Describing shapes

Classroom technique: Barrier game

Thinking about shapes
Children need to experience and talk about a wide range of shapes – not just regular triangles and hexagons sitting on their bases. This activity helps children look carefully at various shapes and think about their properties.

Language
This introduction gives you the opportunity to model useful vocabulary, both mathematical and informal.

Barrier game
Some children may be able to work sitting back to back; others may prefer to use a large book or sheet of card as a barrier.

Introduction

Give out RS23 and display the resource sheet. Describe one of the shapes and ask children to put a coloured counter on that shape – for example, "Put a red counter on the long thin triangle that is pointing down."

Allow the children to ask questions to clarify your meaning: "Is that the one near the top of the paper?"

Invite one or more children to take a turn at describing a shape to put a counter on, supporting them as necessary.

Finally, ask children for words that might be useful in describing the shapes and scribe them on the board, leaving them up for children to look at during their independent work.

corner	triangle	rectangle
square	right angle	pentagon

(m) *Put a green counter on the wide pentagon, the one that looks like a house upside down.*

(speaking) *What can you tell the class about your shape? How many sides and angles does it have?*

Pairs

Children work in pairs with a copy of RS23 each and some coloured counters. They sit with their back to their partner.

Children do a similar activity to the one in the introduction, taking turns to put a coloured counter on one of the shapes and describing which one it is so their partner can put a counter on that shape on their sheet. They compare their work and correct any discrepancies, then continue.

About ten minutes before the end of the session, children can repeat the activity, using coloured pens to colour in their shapes: "Colour the diamond yellow."

(m) *When Alice tells you where she has put her counter, what do you see in your head?*

👤 *If you are not sure which shape Chris wants you to put your counter on, what can you ask him?*

😊 *How far did you get before you felt you needed to compare your sheets?*

Support: Children check the position of each counter after it is placed.

Extend: Children complete the whole sheet without viewing each other's work.

Plenary

Remind children of the maths and speaking and listening objectives of the lesson: write them up and briefly discuss what they mean and how they relate to what the children have been doing.

> Use mathematical vocabulary to describe 2D shapes.
>
> Give accurate instructions.

Self-evaluation
Encourage children to think about how often they needed to compare sheets with their partner and how many, or few, discrepancies they found when they did so.

Give children a minute to think about how they have achieved at each objective, then another two minutes to share these thoughts with their partner.

👤 *How difficult was it to describe the shapes?*

👤 *Which shapes were easy to describe? Which weren't?*

😊 *How hard did you work today? How much did you try?*

Assessment for learning

Can the children

🅜 Use appropriate vocabulary to describe simple 2D shapes?

👤 Recognise whether they have given enough information to identify a particular shape?

😊 Name one thing they have done well and another where there is room for improvement?

If not

🅜 Note what words are not being used and plan teaching to focus on the vocabulary and ideas.

👤 Set up activities where you give children inadequate information so that they need to ask questions to establish the missing data.

😊 Work with the class to draw up a short list of possible achievements and ask children to assess themselves on each one. Make sure you give children realistic but gentle assessments of their achievement.

Drawing maps
Classroom technique: Talking partners

Learning objectives

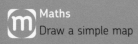 **Maths**
Draw a simple map

Speaking and listening
'Reach an understanding with your partner'
Reach a common understanding with a partner

Personal skills
'Work well with others'
Work with others: work cooperatively with others

Words and phrases
where, position, direction, left, right, in front, behind, next to, beside, map

Resources
paper and pens
glue
scissors

Organisation
Do this introduction in the hall or playground.

Positional language
Introduce the words you want children to use later in the lesson: 'left', 'right', 'in front of', and so on.

Actual objects
Optional: Children collect reminders of what is in front, behind, left or right to add to the map they will make: gravel, leaves, grass, a flower petal.

Tell your partner
Using this technique (p10), encourage children to turn to the other members in their group and agree an answer with them.

Working with others
If necessary, hold a mini-plenary to discuss how to work harmoniously together.

Introduction

Label pairs of children A and B. Child A stands still, and Child B moves to various positions in relation to their partner, according to your instructions.

After a while, children swap roles.

In addition, invite children to take over your role and give instructions.

Stand next to your partner. Stand in front of them, facing them.

How can you describe where Oliver is standing?

Groups of three

Children walk around the school hall or playground and decide on one area. One child stands still, facing in any direction. The other two make notes on paper of what is in front, behind, left and right of that child.

The child standing still can decide at any point to swap roles with another member of their group.

Children return to the classroom and work together to make a simple map of the child and surroundings.

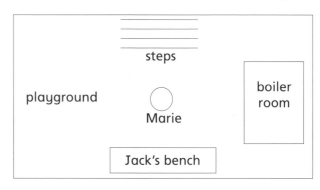

If Mohammad turns round, will the tree still be behind him?

Do you all agree that you should draw the boiler room there?

Who drew what on this map?

Reach an understanding with your partner

Support: Help children with left and right by writing L and R on a large sheet of paper. The child stands in the middle of the large paper with L to the left and R to the right.

Extend: Children add more objects to their maps and try to show their relative positions with some degree of accuracy.

Plenary

Display several of the children's maps, one at a time, and ask questions about them, focusing on direction.

(m) *On this map, what is to the left of Maayan?*

(m) *How would Maayan have to turn to face the tree?*

Assessment for learning

Can the children

(m) Draw a simple map, showing objects in four directions relative to the child in the middle?

(🗨) Talk about a part of the map they did not draw themselves?

(☺) Explain who did what part of the shared task?

If not

(m) Return to the site which is shown on another group's map and discuss how the map represents the buildings and objects in the four directions. Ask children to make simple scenarios with small-world figures and draw what they look like from above.

(🗨) Do some activities using 'Rotating roles' (p10), which formalises the roles taken by each member of the group and ensures equal involvement.

(☺) Ask other members of the group for their opinions and check whether the child agrees or disagrees with these.

Using symmetry
Classroom technqique: Rotating roles

Learning objectives

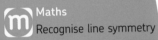 **Maths**
Recognise line symmetry

Learning objectives

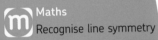 **Maths**
Recognise line symmetry

Speaking and listening
'Join in a discussion with a small group'
Contribute to small-group discussion

Personal skills
'Work well with others'
Work with others: work cooperatively with others

W **Words and phrases**
mirror image, reflection, axis/line of symmetry, symmetrical, the same, explain, convince

r **Resources**
large cut-out equilateral triangle
enlarged versions of six cards from RS25
RS26
for each group:
cards cut from RS25
copy of RS26
mirrors
three labels cut from RS24
paper and pencil
1–3 dice

Tell your partner
To familiarise children with using the relevant language, make statements about what you are doing. Children turn to their neighbour and repeat what you said: "I'm folding the triangle along an axis of symmetry"; "Mrs Taylor is folding ..."

Role labels
Use the labels as they are or attach them to headbands.

Sharing work
Although each child has their role, encourage them to help each other and comment on each other's work.

Symmetry
Check that children understand they are not looking for cards showing a symmetrical shape but for pairs of cards whose shapes can be combined to make a symmetrical shape.

1, 2, 3
Explain that you will be using this adjusted technique (p12) in the plenary to decide which member of a group speaks, so all should be prepared to give an explanation.

Introduction

Show the class a large equilateral triangle cut from paper. Demonstrate that this can be folded in half so that one side, when unfolded, is the mirror image of the other. Talk about the fold line as the line, or axis, of symmetry.

Cut the triangle along the axis of symmetry. Children show how to position what is now two triangles so that these are mirror images of each other.

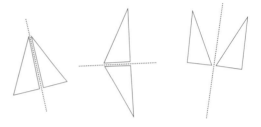

m *Can you show us a line of symmetry in this triangle? Are there any others?*

m *How can we be sure that this is an axis of symmetry?*

Groups of three

Each group of children has a mirror and a set of cards cut from RS25, shuffled and placed face down on the table. Each child has a label cut from RS24 to remind them of their role.

Child A turns over a card and puts it in the centre of the table. Child B checks whether the two shapes form a symmetrical pair, using a mirror. If they find a pair that is symmetrical, Child C draws this pair on plain paper.

After each pair of symmetrical shapes has been recorded, children rotate roles and labels. When all cards are turned over, children check that no more pairs can be formed and agree an explanation of why the remaining cards do not form symmetrical pairs.

m *What different shapes did you make into symmetrical pairs?*

Do you agree that those two cards make a symmetrical shape?

Are you agreeing about when to swap roles?

Support: Before doing the main activity, children look at all cards, match symmetrical pairs and record these pairs of shapes on RS26.

Extend: Children create further pairs of shapes (some pairs symmetrical and some not), using RS26 to record them.

Plenary

Present enlarged versions of the six cards that do not form symmetrical pairs (the right-hand three on the bottom two rows of RS25).

Invite groups to come to the front. Roll a dice to decide who speaks and ask children to pick two cards showing the same shape and explain how they know the pair is not symmetrical.

Can these cards be arranged to make a symmetrical shape?

Convince me that this is not symmetrical.

Assessment for learning

Can the children

Identify and combine a pair of cards to make a symmetrical shape?

Correct a member of their group when they make an error, explaining why they disagree?

Take turns amicably?

If not

Do some work folding and cutting paper, then opening it out to look at the shapes made, using a mirror to observe the reflections.

Provide opportunities for children to correct you when you make deliberate mistakes and encourage them to try to explain those mistakes.

Consider swapping members of the groups. Use plenty of praise to reward any turn-taking that is done with grace.

Identifying shapes
Classroom technique: Tell your partner

Tools
This can be done with an interactive whiteboard, display plastic shapes or a blank flipchart page (draw two shapes and erase the joint edge lines).

Tell your partner
If children are stuck, encourage them to discuss possibilities with their partner before drawing the shapes.

Overcome difficulties
If children find this difficult and make mistakes, suggest they try to draw the combined shape first, then work out where the join may be. You could also give children time to draw the two separated shapes, once you have revealed them.

Introduction

Show two shapes with the sides touching, or two overlapping shapes, so that they appear as one shape.

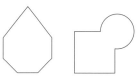

Children draw what they think the two shapes are on wipe boards, then turn to their partner and discuss what they have drawn.

Reveal and discuss the shapes.

(m) *What are the names of the two shapes?*

(speaking icon) *Can you tell us something about the property of the shapes?*

(speaking icon) *Why did you think it was those shapes? Can you draw in the line where the shapes join?*

Pairs/Whole class

Ask a child to help you select two shapes in secret and display them as before. The rest of the class draw what they think the two shapes are and discuss this with their partner.

Children name the shapes on their wipe boards or describe one property of their shape. Collect in names of shapes and descriptions on the board for children to refer to.

> **Shapes**
> circle   octagon   triangle   square
>
> **Words to describe shapes**
> straight sides   curved   eight sides   three corners
> like a square, with its corners chopped off

Your helper decides when the class should show their boards to you and helps you choose a child to come to the front and choose the new shapes.

(m) *If the shape has five sides, can it be a hexagon?*

⬚ *Now you can see the two shapes, tell your partner about them.*

⬚ *Count the sides of your shape and check they are the same as the shape on the screen.*

Support: Arrange pairs so that children needing support work with a more confident child.

Extend: Children use more than two shapes. As a follow-up, children draw around two or more combined shapes and challenge a partner to work out the originals from the outline.

Plenary

Reveal part of a familiar 2D shape. Children give you a 'thumbs up' only when they think they recognise the shape. Ask one or two children for their ideas: accept answers neutrally, but check why the child thinks it is that shape.

Continue to reveal the shape a little at a time, asking for guesses and justifications. Once the shape is revealed, list the properties of the shape as stated by different children.

 square   right-angle corners

four sides   straight sides

ⓜ *How is a square different from an oblong?*

⬚ *Why do you think the shape is what you have just said?*

Assessment for learning

Can the children

ⓜ Recognise and name some 2D shapes?

⬚ Talk with their partner about shared work?

⬚ Keep trying to work out what two shapes are, even when they find it difficult?

If not

ⓜ Do some work spotting the odd one out among a set of rectangles, hexagons or triangles. This can help children focus on the defining characteristics of shapes.

⬚ Set up paired and small-group activities which require children to speak in turn.

⬚ Praise and reward children who persistently try to get over difficulties. Work to develop a class ethos of 'having a go', without worrying too much if they don't succeed.

Self and peer assessment

Lesson 21: Describing shapes	I think	My partner thinks
(m) **I know the names of some shapes.**	🙂 ☹️	🙂 ☹️
🗣️ **I can describe shapes.**	🙂 ☹️	🙂 ☹️

Lesson 22: Drawing maps	I think	My partner thinks
(m) **I can draw a simple map.**	🙂 ☹️	🙂 ☹️
🗣️ **I talk to my group about what we are doing.**	🙂 ☹️	🙂 ☹️

Name _____

Lesson 23: Using symmetry	I think .	My partner thinks
(m) I recognise when a shape is symmetrical.	🙂 ☹️	🙂 ☹️
(head) I talk about my ideas with my group.	🙂 ☹️	🙂 ☹️

Lesson 24: Identifying shapes	I think	My partner thinks
(m) I know the names of some 2D shapes.	🙂 ☹️	🙂 ☹️
(head) I talk about our work with my partner.	🙂 ☹️	🙂 ☹️

Self and peer assessment

Resource sheets

RS5

Name _____

fifty-eight	58	seventy-eight	78
sixty-five	65	nine	9
one	1	ninety-seven	97
twenty-two	22	forty-four	44
twelve	12	sixty-seven	67
fifty-two	52	seventy-one	71
ninety-nine	99	fifty-seven	57
thirteen	13	thirty-one	31
ninety-one	91	nineteen	19
eleven	11	three	3

RS6

Player's name	Hundreds	Tens	Ones

Player's name	Hundreds	Tens	Ones

RS7

Player's name	Tens	Ones

Player's name	Tens	Ones

RS8

Player's name	Thousands	Hundreds	Tens	Ones

Player's name	Thousands	Hundreds	Tens	Ones

Name _____ RS9

1	2	3	4	5	6	7	8	9	10
11									20
									30
31									
									50
51									
									70
71									
									90
91									

Maths Out Loud Year 2 — Lesson 8

Name _____ RS10

1	2	3	4	5	6	7	8	9	10
11									20
									30
31									
									50
51									
									70
71									
									90
91									100
101									110

Maths Out Loud Year 2 — Lesson 8

Name _____ RS11

Maths Out Loud Year 2 — Lesson 9

Name _____ RS12

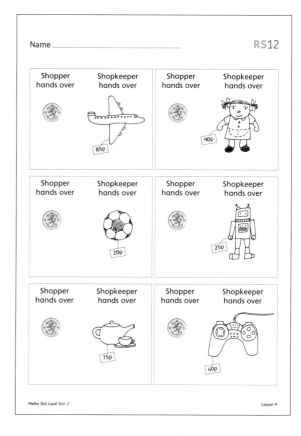

Maths Out Loud Year 2 — Lesson 9

RS13

Name _____

RS14

Name _____

Which table?					Odd one out			
50	100	10	40		60	25	90	40
4	18	8	20		50	10	21	30
50	30	40	20		3	12	6	4
2	12	6	8		18	7	20	8
18	16	20	2		30	90	99	40
30	50	20	10		12	16	9	4
4	2	14	16		50	20	10	31
20	10	90	70		8	6	12	19

✂ -

Which table?

50	100	10	40	(10× table)
4	18	8	20	(2× table)
50	30	40	20	(10× table)
2	12	6	8	(2× table)
18	16	20	2	(2× table)
30	50	20	10	(10× table)
4	2	14	16	(2× table)
20	10	90	70	(10× table)

Odd one out

60	25	90	40	(10× table – 25 is the odd one out)
50	10	21	30	(10× table – 21 is the odd one out)
3	12	6	4	(2× table – 3 is the odd one out)
18	7	20	8	(2× table – 7 is the odd one out)
30	90	99	40	(10× table – 99 is the odd one out)
12	16	9	4	(2× table – 9 is the odd one out)
50	20	10	31	(10× table – 31 is the odd one out)
8	6	12	19	(2× table – 19 is the odd one out)

RS15

Name _____

1	2	3	4	5	6	7	8	9	10
11	12	13	14	15	16	17	18	19	20
21	22	23	24	25	26	27	28	29	30
31	32	33	34	35	36	37	38	39	40
41	42	43	44	45	46	47	48	49	50
51	52	53	54	55	56	57	58	59	60
61	62	63	64	65	66	67	68	69	70
71	72	73	74	75	76	77	78	79	80
81	82	83	84	85	86	87	88	89	90
91	92	93	94	95	96	97	98	99	100

RS16

Name _____

The whole (how many cubes in the stick?)	Can you halve it?	If so, how many in each half?

RS17

Maths Out Loud *Year 2*   Lesson 13

RS18

Name _____

1. Choose one of these titles for the graph and write it at the top.
   • Vehicles that passed Bellfield School last night
   • Vehicles parking in Bellfield School yesterday
   • Vehicles Mr Jones used when he was on holiday

2. Choose five types of transport.
   Write them along the bottom axis of the graph.

| taxi | car | lorry | milk float | bicycle |

| fire engine | bus | tractor | van | motorbike |

3. Make up three questions about your graph.

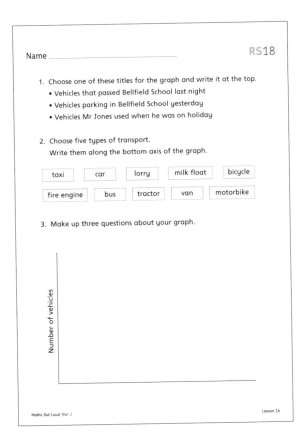

Number of vehicles

Maths Out Loud *Year 2*   Lesson 16

RS19

Name _____

Dear Children,
I hope you can help me. I have lost
my knife and my spoon and only
have a fork left. This is how big it is.
Can you draw a knife and spoon
the correct size for me, so that I can
ask my friend, the blacksmith, to
make me some new ones?

Thank you and best wishes from
Mrs J Giant

Maths Out Loud *Year 2*   Lesson 18

RS20

Name _____

Dear Children,
I hope you can help me. I have lost my
knife and my spoon and only have a
fork left. The fork is 28 cm long. Can you
draw a knife and spoon the correct size
for me, so that I can ask my friend, the
blacksmith, to make me some new ones?

Thank you and best wishes from
Mrs J Giant

Maths Out Loud *Year 2*   Lesson 18

Name _____ RS21

Month _____

Monday	Tuesday	Wednesday	Thursday	Friday	Saturday	Sunday

Maths Out Loud *Year 2* Lesson 19

Name _____ RS22

These facts are true:

This man is nearly 2 metres tall.

This ruler is 30 centimetres long.

This bag of sugar weighs 1 kilogram.

This apple weighs 150 grams.

This is 1 litre of juice.

This is 200 millilitres of juice.

Which of these facts do you think are true?

This book weighs 500 kilograms.

This magazine weighs 400 grams.

This carton of milk holds 500 millilitres.

This carton of milk holds 500 litres.

This tree is 20 centimetres tall.

This pencil is 20 centimetres long.

Make up some statements of your own.

Which of these facts do you think are true?

_____

_____

_____

_____

_____

Maths Out Loud *Year 2* Lesson 20

Name _____ RS23

Maths Out Loud *Year 2* Lesson 21

RS24

I turn the cards over.

I check whether the two pictures are symmetrical.

I record our work.

Cut out the labels and use them as they are or attach them to headbands.

Children each have a label to remind them of their role, then, after each new pairing of cards, rotate them.

Maths Out Loud *Year 2* Lesson 23

RS25

RS26